Censorship
A Beginner's Guide

ONEWORLD BEGINNER S GUIDES combine an original, inventive, and engaging approach with expert analysis on subjects ranging from art and history to religion and politics, and everything in between. Innovative and affordable, books in the series are perfect for anyone curious about the way the world works and the big ideas of our time.

Beginners GUIDES

Censorship
A Beginner's Guide

Julian Petley

ONEWORLD

OXFORD

A Oneworld Paperback Original

Published by Oneworld Publications 2009

Copyright © Julian Petley 2009

ISBN 978–1–85168–674–2

Typeset by Jayvee, Trivandrum, India
Cover design by www.fatfacedesign.com
Printed and bound in Great Britain by Bell & Bain, Glasgow

Oneworld Publications
185 Banbury Road
Oxford OX2 7AR
England
www.oneworld-publications.com

Truth and understanding are not such wares as to be monopolised and traded in by tickets and statutes and standards. We must not think how to make a staple commodity of all the knowledge in the land, to mark it and license it like our broadcloth and our woolpacks.

John Milton, 1644.

Who would overthrow the liberty of a nation must begin by subduing the freedom of speech.

Benjamin Franklin, 1722.

If liberty means anything at all, it means the right to tell people what they don't want to hear.

George Orwell, 1945.

Freedom of expression constitutes one of the essential foundations of a democratic society and one of the basic conditions for its progress and for each individual's self-fulfilment. It is applicable not only to information or ideas that are favourably received or regarded as inoffensive or as a matter of indifference, but also to those that offend, shock or disturb. Such are the demands of pluralism, tolerance and broad-mindedness without which there is no democratic society.

European Court of Human Rights, 1976.

For Mary

Contents

Introduction

Think of censorship, and you may well conjure up the image of some grey bureaucrat in a dusty office snipping at away at a roll of film, or laboriously crossing out words and lines on a printed page. You may also imagine this scene playing out in the past – in Nazi Germany or Stalin's USSR perhaps – or in one of today's authoritarian societies such as Burma or Saudi Arabia. And indeed this book is partly about censorship in the past, and does partly concern itself with censorship in undemocratic regimes. But it is also very much about the present, about the censorship of the latest forms of communication, and about how censorship exists in democracies too. For even in such societies, freedom of expression is never absolute.

In a book of this length, indeed of any length, it would clearly be impossible to give a complete history of censorship in all its forms across the globe and throughout history. Those in search of such an account are advised to turn to Derek Jones's monumental, four-volume *Censorship: a World Encyclopedia*,[1] which runs to nearly 3,000 densely packed pages. Instead, this book presents an account of the main *forms* of censorship to be found in the modern world, illustrating by means of examples how they actually work and how they developed. It is based on the premise that in order fully to understand how the freedom of the media is circumscribed, we need to define censorship in a broad sense so as to include not only the activities of governments and the effects of laws but also the operations of regulators of one kind or another, the workings of market forces, and indeed more nebulous but nonetheless extremely important factors such as the ideological tenor of the times. Derek Jones usefully defines censorship as 'a variety of *processes* … formal and informal, overt and covert, conscious and unconscious, by which restrictions are imposed on the collection, display, dissemination, and exchange of information, opinions, ideas, and imaginative expression',[2] and this book will explore the operations of forms of censorship from this broad perspective.

The book is organised so that it proceeds from an examination of the most direct forms of censorship to those which operate in more indirect and covert ways. We thus start with the murder and intimidation of journalists, an ever-growing phenomenon and one which is causing growing concern across the world. In war zones, journalists are increasingly excluded unless they choose to be 'embedded', and those who do manage to report 'unofficially' or independently are increasingly regarded as legitimate targets. In authoritarian countries, journalists who offend against powerful political, corporate or criminal interests are attacked with impunity – Russia furnishing a particularly acute example of this tendency – and even in democratic countries such as the UK, police harassment of journalists covering demonstrations has reached such a pitch that it has been the subject of protests by the National Union of Journalists and debate within the European Parliament. The consequence, and indeed the purpose, of all such forms of intimidation is to prevent or at least discourage the journalistic investigation of certain topics. This is the most direct and dramatic form of censorship at work in the world today, and it is on the increase.

The destruction of works of art and literature performs a similar function. Not only does it constitute a highly symbolic attack on the values and belief systems represented by the works in question, but it also sends out a powerfully intimidatory message to the creators and owners of such works. As the German poet Heinrich Heine so presciently warned in 1823: 'Wherever they burn books, they will end up burning people', an admonition all too clearly borne out by the Holocaust but which also finds an echo in the events surrounding *The Satanic Verses*, the Danish cartoons and *The Jewel of Medina*. (These are explored both in chapter 1 and the Conclusion.)

A less dramatic, but still effective, form of censorship is to draw up lists of banned works and to forbid people both from publishing and accessing them. This form of censorship is discussed in chapter 2. The most famous of these lists was the *Index Librorum Prohibitorum* of the Roman Catholic Church. This was finally abandoned in 1966, but it is not exactly difficult to find examples of indexes in the modern world – for example the lists of IPs and URLs which help to constitute the Great Firewall of China, the blacklist operated in Britain by the Internet Watch Foundation (both discussed in chapter 5), or the list of 'video nasties' drawn up by the Director of Public Prosecutions in Britain in the early 1980s (chapter 4).

Of course, the most effective form of censorship consists in preventing contentious material from ever being produced in the first place. This is a particular specialism of authoritarian societies, where the absence of democratic structures makes such a degree of control possible. For example, in the Third Reich, everybody who worked in the cultural and communications fields had – if they wished to work at all – to belong to the appropriate chamber of the Reich Chamber of Culture, which in turn was attached to the Ministry of Propaganda, and to abide strictly by its numerous rules. Thus, at a stroke, it was possible to exclude Jews, Socialists, Communists and everyone else deemed 'undesirable' from the realms of the arts, culture and the media, and to ensure that those remaining obeyed the rules, of which there were many. Hence, except in the first two years of the regime, there was, paradoxically, relatively little censorship (in the sense of cuts and bans of completed works) in one of the most authoritarian regimes of the twentieth century. However, this aspect of Nazi *Gleichschaltung* (co-ordination) is, in the last analysis, a particularly extreme and virulent form of media control practised in democratic countries too, namely, licensing.

Licensing is a system by which the authorities grant permission to certain bodies to operate in the marketplace, and is meant to ensure that only works which are produced and/or approved by these organisations are allowed into circulation. Chapter 2 examines the origins of this idea in the licensing of the press, which began in England in the sixteenth century and lasted until the end of the seventeenth. Of course, this being a democracy, the system of control was far from watertight and was eventually abandoned (albeit in favour of other forms of control), but it still furnishes an instructive example of what we might call the will to censor. Far more effective was the licensing of the English stage, which originated in the fifteenth century and persisted well into the second half of the twentieth, and which demonstrates the really quite remarkable extent to which, even in the modern era, the authorities were prepared to go in order to circumscribe the topics with which plays were allowed to deal.

Those who never experienced English theatre censorship at first hand may be surprised that such a degree of moral control could still be exercised even in the 'Swinging Sixties', but chapters 4 and 5 show that licensing exists in modern times too by examining in some detail a form with which every reader of this book will be familiar – that of films, whether on video/DVD or in the cinema. The chapters take pains to emphasise the differences between the US and UK licensing systems, in particular the different role which the state plays in each, but also their similarities. In particular they show how, unlike in authoritarian societies, the licensers have been forced to take account, albeit frequently unwillingly, of changing public tastes and standards. But as in the case of theatre censorship in England, what is particularly notable about each is the role played by overtly moral concerns about cinematic content (see in particular pp. 53–9) which, in the British case, were also allied to specifically political ones (pp. 80–4). These in turn were based on more general fears about cinema's alleged ill-effects (pp. 47–9, pp. 85–7), and such fears still underpin many arguments for the censorship of various media in modern societies, the most recent target being the Internet, which is discussed in chapter 5. 'Media effects' are a highly contentious topic, but those interested in exploring it further are recommended Barker and Petley, Gauntlett, and Millwood Hargrave and Livingstone.[3]

The chapter on the British system of licensing films concludes that it is in fact less independent of the state than is generally supposed, while the chapter on the US system suggests that, in the last analysis, it represents a form of economic censorship. In short, American film-makers do not have to submit themselves to the licensing process (as they do in Britain), but if they refuse to do so, they may find it impossible, or extremely difficult, to get their films shown in mainstream cinemas or sold/rented by the major DVD chains. This then leads, in chapters 5 and 6, to further discussion of various forms of what has come to be known as market censorship. This is admittedly harder to pin down than state censorship (which at least has the virtue of being overt and direct) but, in that it narrows the range of media content on offer, elevates entertainment over information, treats audiences as consumers rather than citizens, puts too much power in the hands of too few media owners, and encourages overly close relationships between governments and media corporations, is coming to be seen by an increasing number of commentators as a peculiarly insidious, systemic form of modern media censorship which denies citizens their full communicative rights (a notion which is discussed in the Conclusion).

Chapter 5 also argues that, contrary to earlier utopian conceptions of the Internet, cyberspace is by no means a censor-free zone, and that coming years are likely to see increasing attempts to control it, not simply in authoritarian countries but in democratic ones too. Leading on from this, the Conclusion suggests that we need to think anew about censorship, and how to combat it, in the twenty-first century. At the start of the 1990s, it was possible to imagine that the media, at least in Europe, faced a future of greater freedom. The collapse of the Communist regimes in Eastern Europe spelled the end there not only of forms of direct state censorship but also made it much more difficult for Western European governments to invoke the Communist bogeyman and 'national security' as pretexts for their own acts of censorship. However, ensuing events were to confound many of these dreams of freedom. Many of the new governments of countries in which free expression had long been confined did not suddenly embrace it with gratitude. Furthermore, with the overnight arrival of a cut-throat brand of 'booty' capitalism, many of the newly democratised Eastern European states awoke to find that their media had been gobbled up by foreign companies. Equally, many of the new private media companies were run by members of the old Communist elite, whose attitude to media freedom, and in particular to the media's relationship with government, remained largely unreconstructed.

And then, with 9/11 and the subsequent terrorist attacks in various European countries, many of the features of the Cold War returned to haunt the European media, with the spectre of Communism being replaced by the shadowy threat of 'Islamic fundamentalism'. Once again, civil liberties – including freedom of expression – have found themselves sacrificed to 'national security' (particularly in the UK, closely identified as it is with American foreign policy). And as the affairs of the Danish cartoons and *The Jewel of Medina* all too clearly show, many in the media came to practice that most insidious form of censorship – self-censorship – particularly when dealing with Muslims and Islam. In some cases this stemmed from a well-meaning (if misguided) desire not to offend religious feelings (the revival of which has been a particularly striking feature of parts of the post-millennial European landscape), but in others merely out of fear of reprisal. But whichever was the case, freedom of expression was the clear loser.

In this not so brave new world, then, we need above all else to reassert the central place which freedom of expression should hold in democratic thought. Without it, democracy itself is in peril. We also need to understand that, even in modern democratic societies, the will to censor is alive and kicking. We also need to recognise that, in some cases it resides within ourselves. This book attempts to show the various forms which this impulse takes, and suggests that although the modern media may be very different from the books which emerged from Gutenberg's printing press, the urge to control them, and indeed some of the means employed to do so, have remained remarkably constant.

1

Death and destruction

Undoubtedly, the most effective way of censoring someone whose views one does not wish to be heard is to kill them, or, failing that, to frighten them into silence. History is, unfortunately, littered with such figures, one of the most famous being Socrates, who was condemned to death in Athens in 399 BCE for his unorthodox beliefs and habits. A more recent example is provided by Steve Biko, who founded the Black Consciousness Movement in South Africa in the late 1960s. His political activities caused him to be banned by the apartheid regime in March 1973, which meant that he was not allowed to speak to more than one person at a time, was restricted to certain areas, could not make speeches in public and could not even be quoted. On 17 August 1977, Biko broke his banning order by visiting Cape Town and was arrested at a police roadblock under the Terrorism Act No. 83 of 1967. Whilst in prison he was repeatedly tortured until, near death, he was transported in a police van 1,500 km to Pretoria, where there was a prison with hospital facilities. He died shortly after arrival on 12 September. In spite of his massive head injuries, the police claimed his death was the result of an extended hunger strike. No prosecutions were ever brought. Biko's story is the subject of Donald Woods' book *Biko* (1978), which formed the basis of Richard Attenborough's film *Cry Freedom* (1987).

Today, however, it is most frequently journalists and those working with them who fall victim to this ultimate form of censorship.

Killing the messenger

On 16 June 2008, the Secretary General of the United Nations, Ban Ki-moon, unveiled a light sculpture on the roof of BBC Broadcasting House in central London. Called 'Breathing', the 10m glass and steel cone projects into the air a beam of light 1km high every night during the BBC's ten o'clock television news bulletin. The memorial's inauguration followed the deaths in Afghanistan of two BBC journalists, Abdul Samad Rohani and Nasteh Dahir Faraah, but is dedicated to all news journalists, and those working with them, who have been killed whilst carrying out their work. As Rodney Pinder, the Director of the International News Safety Institute (INSI), which co-hosted the event with the BBC, put it: 'These men and women are the unsung heroes of democracy, for without a free press there can be no freedom. This shaft of light in the capital of international journalism is a visual reminder of their sacrifice', whilst the BBC Chairman Sir Michael Lyons said: 'We are all reminded of the daily risks taken by journalists in some of the world's most dangerous places. The implicit contract, whereby journalists place their lives at risk to help us understand the world and its events better, needs to be reaffirmed at moments like this'.

Threats to journalists, and not simply to those working in war zones, are now so severe worldwide that on 23 December 2006 the United Nations Security Council unanimously adopted resolution 1738 which 'condemns international attacks against journalists, media professionals and associated personnel', reminds member states that, under the 1949 Geneva Conventions and their two additional protocols of 1977, such workers 'engaged in dangerous professional missions in areas of armed conflict shall be considered as civilians and shall be respected and protected as such', and reaffirms the need to bring to justice those involved in attacking them. Interestingly, the US has signed, but not ratified, the 1977 protocols.

Of course, war zones are extremely dangerous, but most journalists killed in such places, particularly Iraq, are deliberately targeted and not the random victims of battlefield fire. Meanwhile the number of journalists killed indiscriminately steadily rises as those involved in conflicts become increasingly reckless with regard to the safety of journalists – for example, the sixteen Serbian journalists who were killed when NATO forces destroyed by bombing the headquarters of Radio Television of Serbia in Belgrade on 23 April 1999 during the Kosovo War. Furthermore, 'classical' war between two or more sovereign powers has now become the exception rather than the rule, and in many contemporary conflicts, particularly those involving militias of one kind or another, it can be extremely difficult to determine who should be held accountable for breaches of the Conventions, let alone to prosecute them for such breaches. In these circumstances it is hardly surprising if some media organisations are unwilling to send journalists to certain war zones, but this inevitably threatens to diminish – and thus to some extent to censor – the global media coverage which these conflicts receive. The alternative – safely to 'embed' journalists with friendly forces – has been accused of running the risk of threatening their independence and objectivity, and thus of introducing a form of self-censorship. Furthermore, if journalists are seen to enjoy a close operational relationship with one of the belligerents in a conflict, this can fatally undermine precisely that perception of neutrality which is the basis of the legal protection for media workers in war zones.

However, by no means all journalists killed in the course of their work have been reporting from war zones. Indeed, quite the opposite. According to a report published by the International News Safety Institute, *Killing the Messenger* (http://www.newssafety.com/stories/insi/globalinquiry.htm), one thousand journalists and support staff died trying to report the news around the world between 1996 and 2006, an average of two a week. However, only one in four news media staff died covering war and other armed conflicts, and the great majority died in peacetime, working in their own countries. At least 657 men and women were murdered during this period, and only one in eight of their killers was prosecuted. Furthermore, in two-thirds of cases the killers were not even identified, and probably never will be, thus underlining the absence of full and proper investigations when a journalist or other news professional is killed. According to the report: 'The top ten bloodiest countries over the past 10 years were Iraq, Russia, Colombia, Philippines, Iran, India, Algeria, the former republics of Yugoslavia, Mexico and Pakistan. Shooting was by far the greatest cause of death, accounting for almost half the total. Bombing, stabbing, beating, torture, strangulation and decapitation were also used to silence reporting. Some men and women just disappeared, their fate unknown'.

In recent times, the most prominent victim of such attacks was Anna Politkovskaya, the special correspondent for the Russian independent newspaper *Novaya Gazeta*, who was well known for her investigative reports on corruption and human rights abuses, not least in Chechnya, and who was murdered on 7 October 2006. Since Vladimir Putin assumed the Russian presidency in 2000, at least twenty journalists, all of whom had angered powerful vested interests, have died in suspicious circumstances. Other high-profile journalists who have been murdered in the course of their work are Veronica Guerin, a reporter for the *Sunday Independent* newspaper in the Republic of Ireland, who investigated and wrote about Dublin's drug trade and was murdered on 26 June 1996, and Martin O'Hagan, who worked for the *Sunday World*, in which he wrote about the criminal activities of the Protestant paramilitary group, the Ulster Volunteer Force. The newspaper's Belfast offices were bombed twice, and O'Hagan himself received numerous death threats. He was murdered by the Loyalist Volunteer Force, a breakaway Loyalist faction, on 28 November 2001. No-one has ever been charged with his murder.

Such instances not only silence their victims for eternity, but they also act, and are intended to act, as a warning to others. Just how commonplace today is this ultimate form of censorship can also be gleaned from the Reporters Without Borders round-up of the state of press freedom worldwide in 2008 (http://www.rsf.org/article.php3?id_article=29797). This showed that in 2008 sixty journalists were killed, 929 were physically attacked or threatened, and twenty-nine were kidnapped. The Asia–Pacific and Maghreb–Middle East regions were the deadliest for the news media. After Iraq (with fifteen journalists killed), the two countries with the highest death tolls were Pakistan (seven) and the Philippines (six). Mexico remained an extremely dangerous place for journalists to work, with four journalists being murdered there. In Africa, the death toll fell from twelve in 2007 to three in 2008, but this was due to the fact that many journalists stopped working there, often going into exile, and to the gradual disappearance of news media in war zones such as Somalia. Nor is violence reserved only for those working in the traditional media; in 2008 a blogger in China was beaten to death by the municipal police whilst filming a demonstration, and around the world forty-five bloggers were physically attacked.

Reporters Without Borders' Worldwide Press Freedom Index 2007 (http://www.rsf.org/article.php3?id_article=24025) showed that Eritrea has the unenviable distinction of coming at the bottom of the league, replacing North Korea. Of the twenty countries at the bottom of the index, seven were Asian (Pakistan, Sri Lanka, Laos, Vietnam, China, Burma and North Korea), five were African (Ethiopia, Equatorial Guinea, Libya, Somalia and Eritrea), four were in the Middle East (Syria, Iraq, Palestinian Territories and Iran), three were former Soviet republics (Belarus, Uzbekistan and Turkmenistan), and one was in the Americas (Cuba). Russia featured at 144th place out of a total of 169.

Within the European Union, the murder of journalists is still relatively rare; however actual or threatened violence directed at journalists is both common and on the increase. On 3 May 2008, World Press Freedom Day, Reporters Without Borders published a report entitled *European Union: Risks Faced by Journalists* (http://www.rsf.org/article.php3?id_article=26769), which revealed a number of disturbing instances of overt intimidation of journalists in Demark, Sweden, Bulgaria, Romania, Hungary, the Czech Republic, Cyprus, Italy, Spain and Northern Ireland. Fittingly, then, on 25 January 2007, the Parliamentary Assembly of the Council of Europe passed a resolution which reminded member states of their legal obligation under Articles 2 and 10 of the European Convention on Human Rights (which safeguard the right to life and the right to freedom of expression respectively) to 'investigate any murders of journalists as well as acts of severe physical violence and death threats against them. This obligation stems from the individual journalist's rights under the Convention as well as from the necessity for any democracy to have functioning media free from intimidation and political threats. Where attacks against journalists can be carried out with impunity, democracy and the rule of law suffer'. It also called upon national parliaments to 'conduct parliamentary investigations into the unresolved murders of journalists as well as attacks and death threats against them, in order to shed light on individual cases and develop as a matter of urgency effective policies for the greater safety of journalists and their right to carry out their work without threats'.

Graven images

Another extreme form of censorship, although one whose target is not people but objects, is iconoclasm: the destruction or mutilation of visual representations of one kind or another, motivated by religion, politics or moral outrage, and carried out either officially on the orders of the authorities or in a less organised fashion by zealous members of the public. That this is a form of censorship is indubitable, and Margaret Aston's remarks about Christian iconoclasm in sixteenth-century England apply equally well to all other forms of iconoclasm: 'When the iconoclasts went to work they were concerned with attitudes as well as objects. They wanted to erase not simply the idols defiling God's churches, but also the idols infecting people's thoughts. They wanted to *obliterate* – mentally and physically'.[1] Such activity has a long history, one which long predates Christianity and is in fact as old as the process of image-making itself. As Aston puts it:

> The defacing (or maiming) of a representation becomes a representative act: the damage to the seen is a way of hurting the unseen. One attacks the physical object in order to destroy the spiritual being that resides in it – or the system of belief to which it belongs. As long as people have believed in gods and fashioned stones in their honour, stone-breaking has held the capacity to effect a spiritual end. Breaking the holy image amounted to breaking a holy power.[2]

In Christian societies, much iconoclastic activity has its roots in the passage in the Book of Exodus which states: 'You shall not make yourself a graven image, or any likeness of anything that is in heaven above, or that is in the earth beneath ... You shall not bow down to them or serve them; for I, the Lord your God, am a jealous God'. In spite of this, the first substantial wave of iconoclasm did not take place in the Christian Church until the eighth century in Byzantium when the emperor Leo III and his successor Constantine V decreed that all images and idols were to be destroyed. The policy was reversed in the following century, however, and the issue did not arise again within

Christianity in any widespread fashion until the Reformation in the sixteenth century, when it returned with a vengeance, especially amongst the followers of Jean Calvin in what are now the Netherlands and Belgium (where the iconoclastic fury was known as the *beeldenstorm*) and in parts of France, as well as in Copenhagen, Wittenberg, Münster, Augsburg, Zürich, Bern, Geneva and Basel. And, all too often, iconoclasm went hand in hand with another form of destruction, as no less than Martin Luther noted in 1525 when he warned that: 'No one who sees the iconoclasts raging thus against wood and stone should doubt that there is a spirit hidden in them which is death-dealing, not life-giving, and which at the very first opportunity will also kill men, just as some of them have begun to teach'.[3]

In England the first wave of iconoclasm took place in the reign of Henry VIII (1509–47), with the first order to parochial clergy to take down certain kinds of images being issued in 1538, in order to avoid 'that most detestable sin of idolatry'. The most spectacular results of this order were the shrine of Our Lady of Walsingham, and that of Thomas Becket at Canterbury. Iconoclasm was supported by Thomas Cranmer, who became Archbishop of Canterbury in 1532, and who, at the coronation of Henry's successor, Edward VI (1547–53), called on the new king to see 'idolatry destroyed, the tyranny of the bishops of Rome banished from your subjects, and images removed'.[4] A series of injunctions issued in 1547 expressed the new king's concern to see 'the suppression of idolatry and superstition throughout all his realms and dominions' and ordered the clergy to 'forthwith take down or cause to be taken down and destroyed' a remarkably wide range of images and objects and indeed to attempt to erase them entirely from popular memory.

This resulted in images in St Paul's and most London churches being smashed. The process continued during the reign of Elizabeth I (1558–1603). Thus in 1559 Archbishop Parker and a number of bishops issued 'A Declaration of Certain

Principal Articles of Religion', Article X of which stated: 'I do utterly disallow the extolling of images, relics and feigned miracles, and also all kind expressing God invisible in the form of an old man, or the Holy Ghost in the form of a dove, and all other vain worshipping of God, devised by men's fantasies'.[5] At Bartholomew's Fair in Smithfield, at St Paul's Churchyard and elsewhere in London and across the country, rood screens and other wooden images were publicly burned.

By the end of the sixteenth century, iconoclasm had become an accepted part of English religious orthodoxy, and from here it was not a great leap to the better known iconoclasm which expressed itself with a particular vengeance during the English Civil War (1642–51) and the Commonwealth period (1649–60), which followed the temporary abolition of the monarchy. Thus, for example, a Parliamentary Ordinance of 28 August 1643 stated that 'all Monuments of Superstition and Idolatry should be removed and abolished', specifying among other things altar rails and steps, crucifixes, crosses, images of the Virgin Mary, pictures of saints and 'superstitious inscriptions', and in May 1644 the scope of the Ordinance was widened to include representations of angels, rood screens, holy water stoups, organs, and images in stone, wood and glass and on plate. A clear picture of what this policy involved in practice is provided by the journal kept by William Dowsing, who was Provost-Marshall of the armies of the Eastern Association during the Civil War. In 1643 he was appointed by their Captain-General, the Earl of Manchester, as 'Commissioner for the destruction of monuments of idolatry and superstition'. He described his work thus:

> [In] Sudbury … We brake down a picture of God the Father, 2 crucifix's, and Pictures of Christ, about an hundred in all; and gave order to take down a Cross off the Steeple; and diverse Angels, 20 at least, on the Roof of the Church … Dunstal …

We brake down 60 Superstitious Pictures; and brake in pieces the Rails; and gave order to pull down the Steps … [At Clare College chapel, Cambridge] we brake down 1000 pictures superstitious; I brake down 200; 3 of God the Father, and 3 of Christ, and the Holy Lamb, and 3 of the Holy Ghost like a dove with wings.[6]

The practice of iconoclasm is not, however, only the preserve of the religious – revolutionaries, too, have a propensity for it, and, ironically, they likewise tend to employ it against religious symbols In France during the Revolutionary period (1789–99), iconoclasm in some places went far beyond the destruction of religious images; numerous churches and abbeys were entirely demolished (as at Cluny, for example, where one the largest churches in Christendom was essentially turned into a stone quarry); the Gregorian calendar (which had been instigated by Pope Gregory XIII in 1582) was replaced in 1793 by the French Republican calendar, which abolished Saints' days and all other days with Christian associations; names of streets and places with Christian connotations were frequently changed (thus St Tropez becoming for a while Héraclée); whilst in Paris, during the period of the Cult of Reason, which flourished from 1792 to 1794, all churches were closed, the holding of Mass was forbidden and several churches were turned into Temples of Reason, including, on 10 November (20 Brumaire) 1793, Notre Dame itself.

When the Russian monarchy was abolished in 1917, its symbols, such as double-headed eagles and statues and paintings of tsars were the object of widespread iconoclastic fury, whilst most churches and cathedrals were either closed or demolished; some, however, were turned into 'museums of atheism', in which religious imagery served exactly the opposite purpose for which it had been created in the first place. Later, Stalinist iconography would quietly disappear from the Soviet Union during the Khrushchev 'thaw' which began in 1956, and later still, with the fall of the Soviet Union in 1991, red stars, imagery of Lenin and all the other visual paraphernalia of communism would be rather more dramatically swept away.

On 16 May 1966, as a result of a power struggle which had been brewing for some time within the Communist Party of China, Mao Zedong launched a campaign to rid China, and in particular the Party, of its 'bourgeois liberal' elements and to speed up and intensify the process of revolutionary change. On 8 August the Party's Central Committee passed its 'Decision Concerning the Great Proletarian Cultural Revolution' (also known as 'The Sixteen Points'), which called for the transformation of 'education, literature and art, and all other parts of the superstructure that do not correspond to the socialist economic base, so as to facilitate the consolidation and development of the socialist system'. The main agents of this revolution, whose most extreme phase lasted until 1969 but which carried on until 1976, were the students known as the Red Guards, who played a key role in the destruction of the 'four olds': old thought, old culture, old customs and old habits. In pursuit of these aims, they destroyed thousands of temples, shrines, tombs and pagodas, ransacking museums and smashing works of art throughout China. Many artefacts were seized from private homes and destroyed on the spot. Books considered to be 'anti-party' – in fact, all foreign and most contemporary Chinese literature – were removed from libraries and bookshops. The Cultural Revolution was particularly devastating for minority cultures in China; for example in Tibet many monasteries were destroyed, often with the complicity of local ethnic Tibetan Red Guards, whilst in Xinjiang province, which is home to the Muslim Uyghur people, copies of the *Quran* and other books treasured by the Uyghur were burned.

In her book *Wild Swans*, Jung Chang movingly reveals this process in microcosm when she recalls what took place at her school:

Being more than 2000 years old, the school had a lot of antiques and was therefore a prime site for action. The school gateway had an old tiled roof with carved eaves. These were hammered to pieces. The same happened to the sweeping blue-glazed roof of the big temple which had been used as a ping-pong hall. The pair of giant bronze incense burners in front of the temple were toppled, and some boys urinated into them. In the back garden, pupils with big hammers and iron rods went along the sandstone bridges casually breaking the little statues. On one side of the sports field was a pair of towering rectangular tablets made of red sandstone, each twenty feet high. Some lines about Confucius were carved on them in beautiful calligraphy. A huge rope was tied around them, and two gangs pulled ... All the things I loved were disappearing. The saddest thing of all for me was the ransacking of the library: the golden tiled roof, the delicately sculpted windows, the blue painted chairs ... Bookshelves were turned upside down, and some pupils tore books to pieces just for the hell of it. Afterward, X-shaped white paper strips with black characters were stuck on what was left of the doors and windows to signal that the building was sealed.[7]

Iconoclasm is also a feature of more recent political turbulence around the globe. Thus, for example, under the Taliban in Afghanistan in 2001, the two massive Buddhas of Bamyan, which were carved into the side of a cliff, were (with considerable difficulty) destroyed by the Taliban on the grounds that they were 'idols' and thus forbidden by Sharia law, along with all other forms of imagery, as well as music, sports and television. On 6 March 2001 *The Times* quoted Taliban leader Mullah Mohammed Omar as stating: 'Muslims should be proud of smashing idols. It has given praise to God that we have destroyed them'. Then, in February 2006, in the wake of the Iraq war, the al-Askari Mosque in the Iraqi city of Samarra, one of the holiest sites in Shi'a Islam, was massively damaged by explosions believed to have been caused by Al-Qaeda in an attempt to foment war between Sunni and Shi'ite Muslims. Although no injuries occurred in the attack itself, at least 165 people are thought to have been killed as a result in the following days, demonstrating the enormous symbolic power which resides in buildings, and thus, equally, in their destruction.

'Pernicious books and damnable doctrines'

This brings us on, finally, to book burning, another symbolic but highly potent expression of the desire to suppress ideas viewed as dissident, to intimidate their progenitors into silence and to whip up the censorious into a self-righteous frenzy of destruction. The best-known examples are probably Girolamo Savonarola's 'Bonfires of the Vanities' and the Nazi conflagrations of May 1933, but unfortunately history is littered with other instances of this practice. Curiously, in the light of the above, one of the earliest instances took place in China at the instigation of the first emperor of the unified country, Qin Shihuangdi, who ruled from 221 BCE to 210 BCE. Convinced that Confucianism was backward-looking and a barrier to progress and that the only sound philosophy was Legalism, he decreed that all Confucian texts, and indeed all those belonging to the so-called Hundred Schools of Thought, be burned. In the end, the only books spared were on practical matters such as agriculture and medicine. Today Qin Shihuangdi is best known for the famous terracotta army with which he was buried, but he is also alleged to have had 460 Confucian scholars buried alive. Significantly, Mao Zedong compared himself to Qin Shihuangdi and is reputed to have claimed that he destroyed a hundred times as many intellectuals as did the first emperor.

During the Roman Empire's last systematic persecution of Christians, the emperor Diocletian issued an 'edict against the Christians' in 303 which ordered the destruction of Christian scriptures and places of worship across the Empire, and prohibited Christians from assembling for worship. Burning was the usual method for destroying the scriptures. However, by 313, Constantine, the first Christian emperor, had announced the toleration of Christianity in the Edict of Milan, and, ironically, it was he who ordered, at the First Council of Nicaea in 325, the burning of the works of the Christian heretic Arius, who questioned traditional notions of the Holy Trinity.

By the seventh century, the Church was carrying out its own burnings of works which it regarded as heretical. A prominent victim was the medieval French theologian Peter Abelard, who also fell out with the authorities over his interpretation of the Trinity, resulting in his being forced to burn his book, the *Theologia 'Summi Boni',* by a synod held in Soissons in April 1121. Hebrew books were regularly consumed by Christian flames in the medieval period; after strictures announced by Pope Gregory IX, Louis IX burned some 12,000 copies of the *Talmud* (one of the central texts of mainstream Judaism) in Paris in 1243, and subsequent Popes such as Innocent IV (1243–54), Clement IV (1256–68), John XXII (1316–34), Paul IV (1555–59), Pius V (1566–72) and Clement VIII (1592–1605) were considerable fanners of the flames.

In 1494, after the overthrow of the ruling Medici family in the wake of the invasion of Florence by Charles VIII of France, a new spiritual and secular leader emerged in the form of the Dominican friar Girolamo Savonarola. Disgusted by what he saw as Florence's excesses of materialism and immorality under the Medicis, he condemned these passionately in his sermons, finding an enthusiastic audience in a population which was demoralised by the Franco-Italian wars, alarmed by a raging epidemic of syphilis and in thrall to apocalyptic millennial fears as the dread year 1500 remorselessly approached. In one of his sermons, he envisaged Christ being carried across the world in a chariot, whose wake was strewn with infidels whose books had been burned and their images smashed. Before long he was urging his followers to build real bonfires – the so-called 'Bonfires of the Vanities'. Artists and collectors were requested to consign voluntarily a variety of precious objects to the flames, and among the many works destroyed were pictures by Botticelli and Lorenzo di Credi, along with books by Ovid, Propertius, Dante and Boccaccio.

Savonarola's targets also included Pope Alexander VI who, on 13 May 1497, excommunicated him. By this time, the inhabitants of Florence were beginning to tire of Savonarola's austere regime, and there was little popular opposition when the Pope issued a warrant for his arrest on the grounds of heresy and sedition. He was tortured, forced to confess, and hanged in chains on 23 May 1498 in the Piazza della Signoria, where one of the 'Bonfires of the Vanities' had taken place. Ironically, his body was then burned, with the ashes being thrown into the River Arno.

Once Johannes Gutenberg invented the printing press around 1450, the Church found it virtually impossible to destroy entire printed editions of works of which it disapproved. Gutenberg's invention played an absolutely key role in spreading the ideas of the Reformation, but, on the other hand, it was with the coming of this Protestant challenge to Rome's hegemony that book burning, along with the iconoclasm noted earlier, became really widespread in Europe. Pope Leo X in 1520 issued the papal bull *Exsurge Domine*, which called for the burning of the works of the 'heretic' Martin Luther (who responded in kind by burning the bull); in Spain, the Supreme Council of the Inquisition ordered that those coming into the country were to be searched for the 'contamination' of his writings which, when found, were publicly burned at autos-da-fé; and in what are now the Netherlands and Belgium, eighty copies of Luther's works were burned at Leuven in October 1520, 400 at Antwerp in July 1521, and 300 in Ghent during the same month. Vernacular versions of the Bible also fell victim regularly to book burning: in 1526, William Tyndale's translation into English of the *New Testament* achieved the dubious distinction of being the first book written by an Englishman to be burned in England, and in Normandy and Provence, pages torn from vernacular Bibles were reportedly stuffed into the wounds and mouths of slaughtered Protestants.

In England, although Luther's works were publicly burned in St Paul's Churchyard in 1521, the sixteenth and early seventeenth centuries were marked as much by the burning of works which questioned the royal succession or the very institution of monarchy itself as by the destruction of works considered heretical. Iconoclasm rather than book burning was the hallmark of the Commonwealth, as noted above, but the Restoration in 1660 saw the burnings of two works by John Milton critical of Charles I – *Eikonoklastes* (1649) and *Defensio Populi Anglicani* (1650). And in the aftermath of the 1683 Rye House Plot to kill Charles II and his brother the Duke of York, the Convocation of the University of Oxford issued a 'Judgement and Decree' against 'certain pernicious books and damnable doctrines, destructive to the sacred persons of princes, their State and Government, and of all Human Society'. This stated that: 'We find it to be a necessary duty at this time to search into and lay open those impious doctrines, which having been of late studiously disseminated, gave rise and growth to these nefarious attempts, and pass upon them our solemn public censure and decree of condemnation'.[8] Among the books burned by this seat of learning were the aforementioned works by Milton and Thomas Hobbes' *Leviathan*.

In the twentieth century, the most notorious book burnings took place in the early days of the Third Reich. On 6 May 1933 students from the Berlin School for Physical Education arrived at Dr Magnus Hirschfeld's Institute for Sexual Science, which was famous for having championed liberal sexual causes such as the legalisation of homosexuality and abortion, running evening classes in sexual education, and building up a comprehensive collection of books, papers and photographs on sexual matters. It was estimated that the collection contained between 12,000 and 20,000 books in 1933. The Nazis poured ink over books and manuscripts, played football with framed photographs and ransacked cupboards and drawers. Four days later, stormtroopers arrived and took an estimated 10,000 books out onto the Opera Square, where they set light to them. Told that the sixty-five-year-old Hirschfeld was abroad recovering from an illness, the stormtroopers replied: 'Then hopefully he'll snuff it without us; then we won't need to string him up or beat him to death'.[9]

Nazi newspapers reported this momentous act of cultural vandalism as 'energetic action against a poison shop' and 'German students fumigate the Sexual Science Institute' run by 'the Jew Magnus Hirschfeld'.

Since the middle of April, students belonging to the *Deutsche Studentenschaft* had in fact been combing libraries and bookshops in order to draw up lists of 'un-German' books to be burned. On 6 May 'fighting committees' of the two main Nazi student organisations, branches of the veterans' organisation *Stahlhelm* (Steel Helmet), SA troopers and police seized the condemned books. The police and the SA also raided private homes. The culmination of this activity took place in Berlin on Unter den Linden, just opposite the University of Berlin, on 10 May 1933, when some 20,000 books were consigned to the flames to the accompaniment of various National Socialist slogans known as the *Feuerspruche* (fire incantations). Thus the works of Marx and Kautsky were burned to the words: 'Against class struggle and materialism; for the national community and an idealistic outlook', and books by Heinrich Mann, Ernst Glaeser and Erich

Kästner to: 'Against decadence and moral decay; for discipline and morality in family and state'; Freud's oeuvre was condemned for its 'debasing exaggeration of man's animal nature'; and Erich Maria Remarque's novel *All Quiet on the Western Front* (a particular Nazi hate-object) was thrown onto the flames 'against literary betrayal of the soldiers of the World War; for the education of the nation in the spirit of literary preparedness'.[10] Other authors whose works were destroyed included Thomas Mann, Arnold and Stefan Zweig, Arthur Schnitzler, Havelock Ellis, Marcel Proust, Andre Gide, Emile Zola, Henri Barbusse, Maxim Gorky, Albert Einstein, Jack London, Upton Sinclair and H.G. Wells. Observing this shameful and shaming event, the Propaganda Minister Josef Goebbels stated:

> The age of extreme Jewish intellectualism has now ended, and the success of the German revolution has again given the German spirit the right of way ... You are doing the proper thing in committing the evil spirit of the past to the flames at this late hour of the night. This is a strong, great, symbolic act, an act that is to bear witness before all the world to the fact that the November Republic has disappeared. From these ashes will arise a phoenix of a new spirit.[11]

Similar 'acts against the un-German spirit' took place on the same day in nineteen university towns across Germany, and eleven others shortly thereafter. Amongst the German authors whose works were regularly consumed by the flames was Heinrich Heine who, in his 1823 work *Almansor*, had all too presciently observed, echoing Luther some 400 years earlier, that 'wherever they burn books, they will end up burning people'.

Shamefully, there was little or no resistance to this campaign. The official organisation of German booksellers swiftly supported the new regime, and across Germany teachers played a key role in 'cleansing' school libraries of unacceptable books.

Thus in the sphere of education, as in so many other areas of German life, the process of Nazi *Gleichschaltung* (co-ordination) was accomplished less by force and terror than by willing and even enthusiastic acquiescence.

Sadly, this barbaric form of censorship did not end with the Third Reich. In the aftermath of the US-backed military coup in Chile in September 1983, troops raided publishing houses and bookshops and burned in the streets of Santiago any books which they found there which they considered dangerous. These included Ariel Dorfmann's anti-imperialist classic *Para leer al Pato Donald* (*How to Read Donald Duck*). They also destroyed the films and equipment of Chile Films, the national film centre, and burned all the books in Quimantù, the Popular Unity government's publishing house. In 1986, at a time of heightened tension, 16,000 copies of Gabriel García Márquez's book *Clandestine in Chile: the Adventures of Miguel Littin*, were publicly burned.

In September 1988, Penguin published Salman Rushdie's novel *The Satanic Verses*. By the end of November it had been banned in several countries, including India, Pakistan, Bangladesh, South Africa, Malaysia and Saudi Arabia. On 2 December it was publicly burned by Muslims in Bolton, and then again in Bradford on 14 January 1989. Malise Ruthven described the latter scene thus: 'Abdul Quddus did the honours: the brown Yorkshireman, tweed overcoated and hatted, the picture of outraged respectability or fascist bigotry, depending on one's point of view, put a match to the book after it had been duly doused in lighter fluid the better to conflagrate. It made a beautiful image, an icon of iconoclastic rage, the perfect emblem for the Rage of Islam, on film, on video, in colour stills, in black and white'.[12] And then on 14 February 1989 the Ayatollah Khomeini issued his famous *fatwa*, proclaiming: 'I inform all zealous Muslims of the world that the author of the book entitled *The Satanic Verses* – which has been compiled, printed and published in opposition to Islam, the prophet and the *Qur'an* – and all those involved in its publication who were aware of its contents are sentenced to death'.

In April two large bookshops in the centre of London, Collets and a branch of Dillons, were firebombed, apparently because they stocked the book, echoing similar attacks on two bookstores in Berkeley, California, the previous February. Not altogether surprisingly, numerous bookshops on both sides of the Atlantic decided not to stock the book. Rushdie was forced into hiding for a decade, the Japanese translator of the book was murdered, the Italian translator beaten up and stabbed, and its Norwegian publisher shot and left for dead. None of the perpetrators of these acts has ever been caught.

Since the *Satanic Verses* affair, fear of giving offence, especially to the religious, has become a major source of the most insidious form of censorship, self-censorship, and we shall return to this topic in the Conclusion.

2
Indexes and licences

Chapter 1 explored the more drastic means of censoring words and images which have already been made publicly available in one form or another. A less violent, but nonetheless extremely effective, form of censorship is simply to forbid certain words and images being made publicly available in the first place. In its most systematic form, such prohibitions take the form of an official list, known as an Index. At best (from the censors' point of view, that is), such strictures can encourage the most effective of all forms of censorship – self censorship – since writers and artists may well be unwilling to spend their time producing works which will never be seen, or which, if somehow seen, will land them in dire, and indeed possibly fatal, trouble with the authorities.

The imprimatur of the Church

The most famous, systematic and comprehensive index of banned works is undoubtedly the *Index Librorum Prohibitorum* established by Pope Paul IV in 1559. However, this was actually preceded by a number of local indexes drawn up in reaction to the fundamental challenges to Catholic doctrine posed by the Reformation, allied with the rapid growth of printing mentioned in the preceding chapter. So, for example, an index was compiled in Lucca in 1545 to prevent distribution of the works of John Wycliff and Jan Hus, and in Venice in 1549 to suppress editions of the Bible 'containing notes and comments opposed to the faith'. In France and the Netherlands it was the universities which took the lead, beginning with the Sorbonne in Paris in 1544 and continuing in Louvain in 1546. The Louvain index was reprinted in 1551 on the orders of the inquisitor-general for Spain, who had a number of Spanish texts added, and local indexes were also drawn up at this time in Toledo, Valladolid, Valencia, Granada and Seville.

The 1559 *Index Librorum Prohibitorum* listed some 550 authors including Boccaccio, Rabelais, Erasmus and Machiavelli in an attempt to 'expunge from human memory the names of heretics'. Sixty-one printers considered as heretics were also listed, and nothing published by them was allowed to be read. In 1564, after the Council of Trent, which was intended to bolster the reform of the Church, Pope Pius IV published the *Tridentine Index*. This drew up ten general rules of censorship which effectively forbade the publication, distribution and reading of all books published by heretics since 1515, unauthorised editions of the Bible, obscene works and books of superstition. In 1571 Pius V established the Congregation of the Index, which was composed of a number of cardinals, and this took on responsibility for the administration of the *Index*, whose proscriptions remained in effect, with modifications, for three centuries. In 1596 Pope Clement VIII issued a new edition of the *Index*. This required printers to send a copy of every new book to the Congregation so that it could receive their seal of approval, the *testamur* (later *imprimatur*). From now on, this index was the only authorised one, and it incorporated many vernacular titles previously listed only in local indexes.

As noted above, the Roman Catholic Church's practice of placing on an index works of which it disapproved had its roots in the challenges posed to its authority by the Reformation in the fifteenth century. However, by the middle of the seventeenth century, the major threats were emanating from Enlightenment thinking, not least in the sphere of the natural sciences. In this respect it is significant that Pope Alexander VII's

Index of 1664 added to the list works by Copernicus, Galileo, Bacon, Hobbes, Pascal, Leibniz, Spinoza and Locke, while that of Pope Benedict XIV in 1758 included Berkeley, Diderot, Hume, Kant, Montesquieu, Rousseau, Gibbon, Defoe, Goldsmith, Richardson and Sterne. By now, however, the sheer number of books being published in Europe was posing considerable problems for the Congregation of the Index.

Nonetheless, in the nineteenth century, in reaction to the spread of literacy and the consequent growth of a new market for works of fiction, a new category of forbidden literature was created: *omnes fabulae amatoriae* (all love stories). Added to the *Index* were works by Flaubert, Balzac, Dumas (father and son), Stendhal, Heine, Hugo and Zola, along with philosophical texts by Comte and Mill. Indeed, by 1881, around 4,000 books were listed. At this point, in the last major revision of the *Index*, Pope Leo XIII decided 'not only to temper the severity of the old rules, but also, on behalf of the maternal kindness of the Church, to accommodate the whole spirit of the Index to the times'.[1] Accordingly he lifted bans on pre-seventeenth century writings; Bibles edited by non-Catholics, as long as these did not impugn the dogma of the Church; obscene works by classical authors (on account of the 'elegance and beauty of their diction'), although young people were allowed to read only expurgated versions. However, still banned were works containing the 'great evil' of heresy, vernacular versions of the Bible, even if translated by Catholics, since 'it has clearly been shown by experience that … more harm than utility is thereby caused, owing to human temerity';[2] obscene books by non-classical authors; attacks on Catholicism; and works that condoned suicide, divorce, duelling and 'other profane matters'. However, the final edition of the *Index*, published in 1948, still contained over 4,000 books and exercised considerable influence over the more traditional of the faithful. The books included all the 'love stories' of Balzac and Stendhal, everything by Anatole France, Hume and Zola, most of Voltaire and D'Annunzio, Casanova's *Memoirs*, Richardson's *Pamela*, Mill's *Principles of Political Economy*, various works by Rousseau including *Emile, Julie* and *The Social Contract*, and Victor Hugo's *Notre-Dame de Paris* and *Les Misérables*. (The 1948 version of the *Index* can be found at http://www.cvm.qc.ca/gconti/ 905/BABEL/Index%20Librorum%20Prohibitorum-1948.htm.)

The *Index* was finally abolished by Pope Paul VI in 1966 following the end of the Second Vatican Council. However, the Sacred Congregation for the Doctrine of the Faith claimed that it still retains its 'moral value' in so far as it appeals to the conscience of the faithful and warns them 'to be on guard against written materials which can put faith and good conduct in danger', and it can still issue an *admonitum* – 'a warning to the faithful that a book might be dangerous. It is only a moral guide, however, without the force of ecclesiastical law'.

'Beleaguered truth'

Banning works once they have been published can be difficult, and often counter-productive, as such bans tend to give the works in question curiosity value, or to draw them to the attention of a public which might otherwise have remained ignorant of their very existence. It is thus actually far more effective to prevent controversial and troublesome works from appearing in the first place. One of the most effective forms of doing this in the early era of the printed word was to licence printers and publishers (who were often one and the same person).

In Britain, such a licensing system was operated in the sixteenth and seventeenth centuries partly via the Stationers' Company. Founded in 1403 and granted a Royal Charter in 1557, this was essentially a guild or trade organisation. Once in possession of its charter it was able effectively to establish a monopoly on publishing, since anyone wishing to publish had to be a member. This had obvious commercial benefits for the company itself (of which it took full advantage), but its members also benefitted from the fact that once one of their number had asserted ownership of a particular work, no other member could publish it. This was the beginning of the notion of copyright. However, the Stationers were also granted considerable powers of censorship by the state, being legally empowered to seek out and destroy works emanating from unlicensed publishers and anything that the authorities deemed subversive or seditious. Those who published unlicensed works could face imprisonment, branding, having their ears cut off and their noses slit. As Christopher Hill has pointed out, the object of censorship in sixteenth- and seventeenth-century England

> was less moral than political and religious, or ideological, corresponding more to censorship in Eastern Europe today than that in England. Its object was to prevent the circulation of dangerous ideas among the masses of the population. Manuscripts, even if unorthodox, could pass from hand to hand among the ruling elite, as they had done before the invention of printing, without serious danger. But when a printed book was put on sale to the general public, authority lost control over it; anyone who had the money could buy it and convey its contents to others. Printing was a sort of 'appeal to the people', it was said after the restoration: that was why it had to be controlled.[3]

The Stationers' powers were further increased in 1586 by a Decree for Order in Printing, which confined printing to London, Oxford and Cambridge. This was issued by the much-feared Court of the Star Chamber which, under the Tudors and Stuarts, was used to suppress opposition to both church and state policies, and in particular to punish those who resisted the imposition of Protestant religious uniformity on every parish in England. In the seventeenth century, however, the Catholic threat to the monarchy was gradually replaced by the Puritan one, and the targets of censorship changed accordingly. In 1637 the Star Chamber greatly intensified the powers of the Stationers, and a new, more complex and far-reaching system of licensing was introduced; the number of authorised printers in London was cut to twenty, unlicensed printers were to be whipped and put in the pillory, imported books were to be vetted by bishops, already-licensed books had to be relicensed before being reprinted, ballads were to be licensed, and no works could be printed without the author's and printer's names, although in actual fact the sheer volume of printing made it impossible to stop the flow of dissident literature, and by 1640 about sixty-five per cent of books published were unlicensed. Then, in July 1641 the Star Chamber, the ecclesiastical courts, the High Commission and the licensing of the press were all swept away by Cromwell's republican revolution. With the end of the monopoly exercised by the Stationers, many of the raw materials utilised in the printing process were suddenly available to independent operators; a flood of books, pamphlets and tracts followed, many of which had been suppressed or circulated only in secret for years. The demise of the printing monopoly also meant that published works became much more easily afford-able. The mood of these revolutionary times was wonderfully captured by John Milton when he wrote:

> Behold now this vast city: a city of refuge, the mansion house of liberty, encompassed and surrounded with his [God's] protection; the shop of war hath not there more anvils and hammers waking, to fashion out the plates and instruments of armed justice in defence of beleaguered truth, than there be pens and heads there, sitting by their studious lamps, musing, searching, revolving new notions and ideas wherewith to present, as with their homage and their fealty, the approaching reformation; others as fast reading, trying all things, assenting to the force of reason and convincement.[4]

However, by the following year, Parliament was already commanding that the 'abuse' of printing be reformed, and the prosecution of publishers began anew. The Stationers' Company, which had never actually been abolished (vested printing interests saw to that) but which was losing money because of the growth of unlicensed presses, petitioned Parliament for a return to full-scale licensing. This was granted in June 1643 by a new Licensing Act which more or less replicated the 1637 measures, except that the new licensers were to be appointed by Parliament. It was this that in 1644 led John Milton, himself a strong supporter of the Puritan revolution, to write his famous defence of freedom of expression, the *Areopagitica*, which was at least partly a response to his unsuccessful attempts to obtain a licence for his writings on divorce which, when published unlicensed, were met with calls in Parliament and the Westminster Assembly for their burning. Needless to say, this argument for 'the liberty of unlicenc'd printing' was published, at some risk to its author, without a licence. It cost 4d a copy.

Nonetheless, it still proved impossible to censor everything of which the authorities disapproved, particularly given the explosive growth of printing and the development of forms of newspaper: from four in 1641 to 722 by 1645. But once the Army effectively took power in 1649 it introduced a Printing Act, which drastically reduced the number of newsbooks (proto-newspapers) in circulation, and these were cut to two by a further Act of 1655. In August 1658, Oliver Cromwell, who had been appointed Lord Protector in 1653, attempted to re-establish effective censorship with his Order for the Control of the Press. Nor were other forms of culture immune from censorship. In 1641 dancing on Sundays was banned, and there followed in 1644 a Sunday ban on masques, feasts, wakes, wrestling, shooting, bowling, and all other sports and pastimes. Maypoles were also banned outright, and London's theatres were closed from 1642 till the restoration of the monarchy in 1660.

This, though, in almost every other respect, saw the return of censorship in nearly all its pre-revolutionary severity. Thus the Licensing Act of 1662 reintroduced the full panoply of pre-publication scrutiny and licensing, but as the range of books published had increased greatly during the revolutionary period, different subject areas were allotted their own specialist scrutinisers. Thus books on history or affairs of state were licensed by a Secretary of State, books on divinity, philosophy and science by the Archbishop of Canterbury, the Bishop of London or the Vice-Chancellor of Oxford or Cambridge. Unlicensed printing was once again forbidden; the number of London printers was reduced to twenty; only four foundries were licensed to cast type; all master printers had to post a £300 surety against any possible future transgression; and every book had to include a facsimile of its licence and the name and address of its printer. The office of Surveyor of the Press was created in 1663 in order to oversee the operations of the Act. Its first incumbent was Sir Roger L'Estrange, who also edited the government-controlled newspaper *The Public Intelligencer*. His attitude to his readers can be gauged from his remark that 'a public mercury [newspaper] should never have my vote. It makes the multitude too familiar with the actions and counsels of their superiors'. Similarly, when he took on the job of Surveyor, he made it abundantly clear that his main target was 'the great masters of the popular style' who 'speak plain and strike home to the capacity and humours of the multitude'.[5]

Again, just how effective was this vast apparatus of censorship is difficult to gauge. Unlicensed works were indeed published, but, equally, many were suppressed and their publishers punished. What seems most probable is that it strongly encouraged self-censorship. So, for example Thomas Hobbes, whose *Leviathan*, was not allowed to be reissued, published none of his serious works on religion and politics which he wrote after the Restoration, his *Behemoth*, which he wrote in 1668, not appearing until 1679 and then only in a pirated edition. A similar fate befell works by Locke, Newton and Samuel Butler.

Finally, in 1695, the Licensing Act was not renewed, and England and Wales became the first European countries to end pre-publication censorship by means of licensing. There were several reasons for this. Firstly, the Stationers' Company had blatantly abused its monopoly over patents and copyrights and had brought the whole system into disrepute. Second, with printing becoming ever easier and cheaper, the licensing system was becoming increasingly difficult to police. Third, licensing was coming to be seen as an unwarranted interference in what had become a profitable business. And finally, the authorities had already begun to find new means of discouraging freedom of expression, in the form of prosecutions for blasphemy, sedition and criminal libel.

'Licentious insolence'

The censorship of plays was originally carried out by the Master of the Revels, a member of the Royal Household answerable to the Lord Chamberlain. The post was created during the reign of Henry VII (1485–1509), and its incumbent supervised the royal festivities, ensuring among other things that nothing offensive to the king was performed. At first his activities were confined to the court, but as theatre became an increasingly widespread form of popular culture, so controls upon it gradually widened and intensified. Within months of her accession in 1558, Elizabeth I had prohibited plays 'wherein either matters of religion or the governance of the estate of the common weale shall be handled'.[6] By the end of the sixteenth century, the duties of the Master of the Revels had expanded to take in licensing the performance of stage plays. Meanwhile the capacity of the London theatres had swelled dramatically; it has been estimated that in the 1590s they were enjoying some 50,000 visits per week, with up to 3,000 people attending a single performance. Inevitably, such popular entertainments, situated as they frequently were in 'low' areas such as Clerkenwell, Blackfriars and Southwark, attracted the suspicion and hostility of the urban authorities, who tended to view these venues as encouraging the spread of not only disease but of lax morals and political subversion.

As noted above, plays largely ceased to be performed during the Cromwellian period, but drama returned in force with the Restoration, well known for its cynical and sexy comedies, although plays were still subject to censorship (but usually on political or religious rather than moral grounds), either by the licensing authorities, in the case of published scripts, or by the Master of the Revels in the case of actual performances.

The activities of the latter took on greater significance when the Licensing Act was finally allowed to lapse in 1695. By this time, reaction against what was seen in some quarters as the immorality of the Restoration stage had set in. In 1699 William III issued a notice to the Master of the Revels 'not to licence any Play containing expressions contrary to Good Manners',[7] and a few years earlier the playwright Thomas Dryden had stated that the Lord Chamberlain's powers embraced 'all that belongs to the decency and Good Manners of the Stage' and that he could 'restrain the licentious insolence of the poets and their Actors that shock the Publick Quiet, or the Reputation of Private Persons, under the notion of "Humour"'.[8]

Nonetheless, the extent to which the Lord Chamberlain and the Master of the Revels could in practice police the stage had its practical limits, and, because certain plays had overstepped the political mark, the Stage Licensing Act was passed in 1737, which for the first time gave the Lord Chamberlain statutory powers. All new plays, and any additions to old ones, had to be submitted to the Lord Chamberlain at least fourteen days prior to their first performance. The number of licensed theatres in

London (in effect the City of Westminster) was reduced. Theatre managers who put on unlicensed plays could be fined £50 and lose their licence. No reason had to be given for withholding a licence from a play, and the Lord Chamberlain's decisions could not be appealed. The Act was strongly opposed by Lord Chesterfield who, in a speech to the House of Lords, argued: 'If poets and players are to be restrained, let them be restrained as other subjects are, by the known laws of their country. A power lodged in the hands of one single man, to judge and determine, without any limitation, without any control or appeal, is a sort of power unknown to our laws, inconsistent with our constitution.[9]

The Act also gave the Lord Chamberlain a helpmate in the form of an Examiner of Plays, who in effect did most of the work. However, it omitted to give either of them any guidance in the matter of what they should or should not allow to be presented on stage. To some extent they thus made up the rules as they went along, although constant preoccupations were satirical attacks on prominent people, and, as the eighteenth century gave way to the nineteenth, moral propriety – hence the tenure of the Examiner George Colman (1824–36) was marked by a complete ban on the apparently indecent word 'thighs'. The first half of the nineteenth century, which was a time of considerable social turbulence, also saw outright bans on the theatrical treatment of subjects such as the Irish problem, Chartism, the extension of the suffrage and the Royal Family. The Lord Chamberlain was particularly concerned about the so-called 'Newgate Dramas', melodramas revolving around crime and appealing specifically to working class audiences. After the examiner had banned one of these in 1853, *The Neglected Child, the Vicious Youth and the Degraded Man*, a member of his staff wrote that 'it is highly desirable to elevate the tone of the drama' adding that this was 'specially necessary in the case of the saloons [minor theatres] who have a tendency to lower the morals and excite the passions of the classes who frequent these places of resort'.[10]

However, the Act contained a number of loopholes and these were effectively closed in 1843 by the Theatres Act, Section 14 of which gave the Lord Chamberlain the power to withhold a licence from a play 'whenever he shall be of opinion that it is fitting for the preservation of good manners, decorum, or the public peace so to do'. Under this system, plays were submitted to the Lord Chamberlain not by the author themselves but by the manager of the theatre wishing to produce it. This encouraged a degree of complicity with the system amounting to a form of self-censorship, as managers' interests were primarily commercial and, in the interests of getting their properties staged as quickly as possible, would frequently do much of the Lord Chamberlain's work for him, negotiating with him about what should be cut or altered, sometimes without reference to the writer. But what is so remarkable about this system of censorship is that, having effectively come into being in 1737, it persisted largely unchanged until 1968. During this time, it acted as a remarkable indicator of the moral, political, social and cultural attitudes of the British Establishment.

'Vulgar, insular prejudice'

In the second half of the nineteenth century, with bourgeois Victorian morality at its zenith, the importation of plays from France which dealt with sexual matters in a relatively light-hearted manner began to exercise the Lord Chamberlain and his Examiner, and *La Dame aux Camélias* by Alexandre Dumas *fils* was banned for many years. Even more problematic were deeply serious plays from the dreaded 'abroad' by playwrights such as Ibsen, whose *Ghosts* was refused a licence in 1891; Sir Ponsonby

Fane, the Lord Chamberlain's Comptroller wrote that the play was 'suggestive of an unwholesome state of things'.

In the early part of the twentieth century, under the influence of continental European playwrights such as Ibsen, a more serious form of theatre had, in spite of the censoriousness of the Lord Chamberlain, begun to develop in Britain, epitomised by the work of George Bernard Shaw and Harley Granville Barker. Both had had plays refused a licence by the Lord Chamberlain, Shaw with *Mrs Warren's Profession*, which concerned prostitution and was banned as 'immoral and otherwise improper for the stage' in 1894 (it would have to be re-submitted four times before it was finally licensed in 1924), and Barker in 1907 with *Waste*, which features adultery and abortion amongst the upper echelons of society. Playwrights such as these began to chafe publicly against the Lord Chamberlain's shackles. For example, on the death of Examiner Pigott in 1895, Shaw referred to him as 'a walking compendium of vulgar, insular prejudice' and continued:

> He had French immorality on the brain; he had American indecency on the brain; he had the womanly woman on the brain; he had the Divorce Court on the brain; he had 'not before a mixed audience' on the brain; his official career in relation to the higher drama was one long folly and panic … It is a frightful thing to see the greatest thinkers, poets and authors of modern Europe – men like Ibsen, Wagner and Tolstoi, and the leaders of our own literature – delivered helplessly into the vulgar hands of such a noodle as this amiable old gentlemen – this despised and incapable old official – most notoriously was.[11]

In Shaw's view, expressed in an American journal in 1899, there was only one thing to be done with censorship: 'Abolish it, root and branch, throwing the whole legal responsibility for plays on the author and manager, precisely as the legal responsibility for books is thrown on the author, the printer and the publisher'.[12]

This, however, was a responsibility which theatre managers by no means wanted. Nor were all playwrights necessarily in favour of such a course of action. Thus testifying in 1909 before a select committee established by the government to examine the issue of stage censorship, W.S. Gilbert (of Gilbert and Sullivan fame) pronounced the not uncommon view that:

> The stage is not a proper pulpit from which to disseminate doctrines possibly of Anarchism, Socialism and Agnosticism. It is not the proper platform upon which to discuss questions of adultery and free love before a mixed audience composed of persons of all ages, of both sexes … of all conditions of life and various degrees of education.[13]

When asked by the committee to explain the principles on which he operated, the Examiner Alexander Redford could reply only: 'Simply bringing to bear an official point of view and keeping up a standard. There are no principles that can be defined. I follow precedent'. However, he also told the committee that 'the stage is not a political arena' and that it was 'not desirable that specially important political questions should be discussed there'.[14]

'Sordid and beastly'

The number of plays banned outright under this system may have been relatively small, but the number of cuts and forced alterations was very considerable indeed. Certain subjects were effectively banned in perpetuity, such as the negative portrayal of the monarchy and of friendly powers – hence bans on plays critical of the Nazis in the 1930s and of the US in the 1960s. The extent of the self-censorship which the system encouraged is quite literally incalculable, since British writers inevitably tended to internalise the standards of the Lord Chamberlain in order to avoid wasting their time writing material which could never be performed. This, of course, is why plays written by continental European or American writers tended in particular to fall foul of the Lord Chamberlain. In doing so, they also very effectively exposed the values which he and his staff brought to their task.

For example, when Strindberg's *Miss Julie*, which had been written in 1888, was presented for licensing in 1927, the then Lord Chamberlain, Lord Cromer, complained of the 'sordid and disgusting atmosphere which makes the immorality of the play glaring and crude'. Worse, 'there is the very questionable theme in these days of the relations between masters and servants'. Other advisers variously objected to the play as 'sordid and beastly', 'filthy' and 'loathsome'.[15] Another continental play to fall foul of Lord Cromer was Pirandello's *Six Characters in Search of an Author*, which was banned in 1925. One of his advisors, Sir Squire Bancroft, who regarded the play as 'plain filthiness', opined: 'This play, I think, comes from Vienna. The sooner it is sent back there, the better. The story they *[sic]* tell is to my mind extremely abominable … To grant a licence for this play would in my opinion be to sanction the performance of a degrading spectacle'.[16]

Even after the Second World War, archaic, philistine and insular attitudes continued to prevail in the world of the Lord Chamberlain. Thus when in 1948 Tennessee Williams' *A Streetcar Named Desire* was submitted, Comptroller Sir Terence Nugent insisted on the removal of Williams' discreet references to homosexuality, and the same happened again in 1955 with his *Cat on a Hot Tin Roof* – of which Chief Examiner Charles Heriot wrote: 'Once again, Mr Williams vomits up a recurring theme of his not too subconscious'.[17] In August 1955, Beckett's *Waiting for Godot* could be performed only in a bowdlerised version. Amongst the censor's many demands were that the words 'Who belched?' were substituted for 'Who farted?'. With *Endgame* in 1958, language was again the problem, the Lord

Chamberlain's office drawing the line at the famous reference to God: 'The bastard – he doesn't exist'. Also excised were the words 'balls', 'arses' and 'pee'. Assistant Examiner Sir Vincent Troubridge regarded the play as 'great nonsense' and 'largely incomprehensible'.[18]

Saved

In the end, though, even the Lord Chamberlain could not withstand the pressure of rapidly changing times. But theatre censorship in Britain did not come to an end without a considerable battle.

By the 1960s, theatres such as the Royal Court, the Royal Shakespeare Company, the National Theatre and Joan Littlewood's Theatre Workshop at Stratford East, which were able to draw on state funding through the Arts Council, were much more prepared than the traditional theatre managers and commercial producers to challenge the Lord Chamberlain's diktats. Bold new writers and ideas were being actively encouraged, and the siege mentality towards continental European culture was finally dissipating. The theatre censor's prudish cuts and niggling changes began to attract an increasing amount of opprobrium, ridicule and resistance.

Plays from abroad such as Jean Genet's *The Screens* and Frank Wedekind's *Spring Awakening* (which had originally been written in Germany in 1891, but was not performed there in its entirety until 1912) continued to meet resistance, with Assistant Examiner Maurice Coles describing the latter as 'one of the most loathsome and depraved plays I have ever read'. However, the two plays which did most to hasten the downfall of the Lord Chamberlain were home-grown: John Osborne's *A Patriot for Me* and Edward Bond's *Saved*, both of which were staged by the Royal Court, the country's most progressive theatre.

The former told the story of the downfall of Alfred Redl, a homosexual Jewish officer in the latter days of the Austro-Hungarian Empire. Homosexuality was a subject which the Lord Chamberlain's office did not like to see treated on stage, and when the play was submitted in 1964, the Lord Chamberlain, Lord Cobbold, stated that he could not license it because of a number of scenes which 'exploit homosexuality in a manner that may tend to have corrupting influences'.[19] In other words, to allow the play to be performed would be to spread the 'infection' of being gay. Rather more forthright was his Chief Examiner Charles Heriot, who deeply disliked Osborne's work and who complained that 'Mr Osborne's overweening conceit and blatant anti-authoritarianism cause him to write in a deliberately provocative way. He almost never misses a chance to be offensive', whilst Assistant Secretary Ronald Hill warned: 'This play looks to me like the Pansies' Charter of Freedom'.[20] In the end, the Royal Court turned itself into a theatre club for the duration of the play's run, thus avoiding bowing to the censor's demands, although the latter claimed that the theatre was engaging in an illegal subterfuge.

On 21 July 1965, the Prime Minister, Harold Wilson, was asked in Parliament about theatre censorship, and he stated that: 'So far as this aspect of national life needs some degree of modernisation, I would have thought there was a pretty strong case here'. Clearly the writing was on the wall for the Lord Chamberlain. And it was at this time that the play which was to prove to be his nemesis arrived in his office. This was *Saved*, by Edward Bond, set in the lower depths of south London, and featuring a scene in which a baby (unseen) is stoned to death in its pram. This early work by one of Britain's greatest (if shamefully underrated) dramatists was described by Charles Heriot as 'a revolting amateur play … The writing is vile and the conception worse'. The list of cuts required ran to four pages, and mostly involved objections to Bond's stark, demotic prose, with demands for the removal of words such as 'arse', 'bugger', 'get stuffed', 'crap', 'piss off' and 'shag', among others. Other instructions stated: 'The couple must not lie down on the couch so that one is on top of the other' and : 'There must be no indecent business with the balloon'.[21] Bond, however, refused to compromise and the Royal Court was again turned into a theatre club in order to present the play. Lord Cobbold complained to the Director of Public Prosecutions (DPP), and also made it clear to the new Home Secretary, Roy Jenkins, that if no legal action were forthcoming he would publicly state that he was being let down by the government. On 6 December, the DPP wrote to Cobbold stating that the Attorney General had agreed to proceedings being instituted against the Court, and on 14 January 1966 a summons was issued under Section 15 of the Theatres Act 1843 for presenting a new play 'for hire' before it had been licensed by the Lord Chamberlain. On 14 February three members of the Court appeared before a stipendiary magistrate and were found guilty. However, Cobbold's victory was a pyrrhic one as, two days later, Lord Annan initiated a debate on theatre censorship in the House of Lords, the upshot of which was that a select committee of both Houses was appointed to examine the issue. When this reported in the autumn of 1967 it unanimously recommended the end of pre-performance censorship in the theatre. In the meantime, the Lord Chamberlain's office carried on as usual, inveighing against another Edward Bond play, *Early Morning*, and the musical *Hair* (criticised by Assistant Secretary Ronald Hill as 'demoralising' and 'dangerously permissive'), which it turned down in three different versions in the final months of its existence

On 26 July 1968 the Theatres Act was given Royal Assent. From now on, the theatre would be subject only to the same laws as other forms of literature, such as obscenity or libel. But as Nicholas de Jongh has rightly observed, the absence of acclaim, in the press and elsewhere, for the abolition of theatre censorship was striking. But, there again, a philistine and deeply conservative press had done its best, from *Ghosts* to *Saved*, to fan the flames of reaction and bigotry which gave the archaic office of the Lord Chamberlain a veneer of legitimacy. Remarkable too, as De Jongh argues, was

> the refusal to blame Lords Chamberlain for the extent of their repressiveness and arrogant philistinism. The damage done by these men was enormous and enduring. They forced the English theatre to cut itself off from depicting and discussing crucial aspects of life with such thoroughness that generations of play-goers came to forget that the theatre could be a forum for expressing political or social protest. Anyone scrutinising the twentieth-century English theatre canon, up to 1968, will be struck by its parochialism, its apparent refusal to concern itself with the greatest issues and anguishes of this violent century, as England, Europe and the world beyond experienced them'.[22]

However, before we console ourselves with the thought that this could have happened only in England, or only in the past, let us turn to forms of licensing which are still very much with us, and which regulate a cultural form far more popular and widespread than the English theatre.

3

Seals and ratings

Censorship of films is very nearly as old as the cinema itself. This is not particularly surprising, as the cinema is a form of popular culture, and the more popular a cultural form, the more likely it is to attract the attentions of the censorious. In spite of the two countries' different attitudes to freedom of expression (and to class), this is as true of the US as of the UK, and this chapter and chapter 4 will explore how a form of licensing developed in each country in order to regulate the contents of cinema films and, in the case of the UK, of videos and DVDs as well.

'Evil effects'

Within months of Thomas Edison premiering his Vitascope on 23 April 1896 at Koster and Bial's Music Hall in New York City, he had hired May Irwin and John C. Rice to perform for the camera their famous lingering kiss from the 1895 Broadway show *The Widow Jones*. The resulting film, lasting forty seven seconds and called quite simply *The Kiss*, featured the first screen kiss in cinematic history, and immediately brought forth howls of outrage from certain quarters. Thus, for example, one contemporary critic wrote: 'The spectacle of the prolonged pasturing on each other's lips was beastly enough in life size on the stage but magnified to gargantuan proportions and repeated three times over it is absolutely disgusting', whilst another fulminated: 'Such things demand police interference. Our cities from time to time have spasms of morality, when they arrest people for displaying lithographs of ballet girls; yet they permit, night after night, a performance which is infinitely more degrading'.[1]

However, as projection equipment became cheaper, and entrepreneurs began to smell a profit, nickelodeons sprang up across American cities, especially in poorer areas. As the films themselves were inflammable, there was concern in some quarters for the patrons' safety, and as their subject matter was considered by some to be risqué, there were worries about their mental health too. By 1910 some twenty-six million people were attending films each week. Local censorship was first intro-duced in 1907 in Chicago, where there were 116 nickelodeons visited by some one hundred thousand customers per day. The *Chicago Tribune* condemned these cinemas for 'ministering to the lowest passions of childhood', and in November 1907 the Chicago City Council passed an ordinance empowering the chief of police to issue permits for the exhibition of motion pictures; a permit could be refused if he felt a film to be 'immoral or obscene, or portrays depravity, criminality or lack of virtue of a class of citizens of any race, colour, creed or religion, or tends to produce a breach of the peace, or riots, or purports to represent any hanging, lynching or burning of a human being'.[2] When two years later the westerns *The James Boys in Illinois* and *Night Riders* were banned, 200 cinema owners sued the city, claiming violation of their constitutional rights. They lost. The court argued that although the film about the James brothers was based on actual events, films that attempt to document such happenings 'necessarily portray exhibitions of crime … [and] … can represent nothing but malicious mischief, arson and murder. They are both immoral, and their exhibition would necessarily be attended with evil effects on youthful spectators'. Chief Justice James H. Cartwright noted that the films were showing in cheap cinemas frequented by children, 'as well as by those of limited means who do not attend the productions of plays and dramas given in the regular theatres. The audiences include those classes whose age, education and situation in life specially entitle them to protection against an evil influence of obscene and immoral representations'.[3]

Because of the growing threat of local censorship of this kind, the People's Institute, a private body concerned with social research and adult education which had already undertaken research into the conditions of motion picture exhibition, suggested the idea of allotting classifications to films. To this end it established an advisory committee which the major film producers' organisation, the Motion Pictures Patents Company, agreed to recognise and support. This committee was called the National Board of Censorship and began work in March 1909. In spite of its name, it was actually concerned less with censorship than with classification and informing audiences about the contents of films, banning only one work (*Every Lass a Queen*) and keeping cuts to a minimum; indeed, it campaigned against federal and state censorship proposals, and concentrated much of its efforts on encouraging the industry to produce better films. In 1916 it changed its name to the National Board of Review and adopted the slogan 'Selection – not censorship – the solution'.

'Mere representations of events'

Meanwhile, though, state censorship was added to local censorship. In 1911 Pennsylvania created the first state censorship board, whose job it was to approve films which were 'moral and proper' and to forbid those which were 'sacrilegious, obscene, indecent or immoral, or such as tend, in the judgement of the Board, to debase or corrupt morals'.[4] Two years later Kansas adopted much the same wording in its censorship statute, whilst the contemporaneous Ohio statute allowed the showing of 'only such films as are in the judgement and discretion of the board of censors of a moral, educational or amusing and harmless character'.[5] Maryland followed suit in 1916. These boards also charged producers for their censorship activities, and in 1915 the Mutual Film Company took the Ohio board to court on the grounds that it was violating both the First Amendment (the constitutional guarantee of freedom of speech) and the Ohio constitution. However, the Supreme Court reached a unanimous decision on the matter which would have serious consequences for local and state-level film censorship in America long into the future. Mutual argued that films were transmitters of information about a wide range of issues, and were therefore entitled to the same freedoms as the press. But the court would have none of it. Judge McKenna argued that films

> may be used for evil, and against that possibility the statute was enacted. Their power of amusement and, it may be, education, the audiences they assemble, not of women alone nor of men alone, but together, not of adults only, but of children, make them the more insidious in corruption by a pretence of worthy purpose or if they should degenerate from worthy purpose … They take their attraction from the general interest, however eager and wholesome it may be, in their subjects, but a prurient interest may be excited and appealed to. Besides, there are some things which should not have pictorial representations in public places to all audiences.

He thus concluded that:

> The exhibition of motion pictures is a business pure and simple, originated and conducted for profit … not to be regarded, nor intended to be regarded by the Ohio Constitution, we think as part of the press of the country or as organs of public opinion. They are mere representations of events, of ideas and

sentiments published or known; vivid, useful and entertaining, no doubt, but ... capable of evil, having power for it, the greater because of their attractiveness and manner of exhibition.[6]

Commercial, purely entertaining and potentially dangerous, the cinema was thus denied the free speech rights vouchsafed to media such as books and newspapers. However, one of the first victims of this ruling was *Birth Control*, a serious and high-minded dramatisation of the work of the family planning pioneer Margaret Sanger, which was banned in New York City in 1917.

As a result of the increasing incidence of local and state censorship, the studios set up in 1916 the National Association of the Motion Picture Industry in order to campaign both for the making of films unlikely to upset the censorious and against local and state forms of censorship. It also established its own censorship committee, and in 1921 this issued the 'Thirteen Points', a list of the kinds of scenes which most frequently fell foul of censorship boards throughout the country. These included nudity, prostitution, gambling, drunkenness and any illicit love affair which 'tends to make virtue odious and vice attractive'. However, as there was no real way of enforcing these provisions, they remained ineffectual. In the same year, however, Florida passed a law requiring cinemas to conform to the ratings of the National Board of Review, and New York State, the country's largest film market, set up its own censorship board. It too used the Pennsylvania wording, but added bans on material which was 'inhuman' or which tended to 'incite to crime'. By the end of 1921, thirty-six states were discussing censorship bills. At the same time as all this censorious activity, film audiences were declining due to a combination of competition from the new medium of radio and a series of epidemics which made people wary of large gatherings.

The Motion Picture Producers and Distributors of America

By now seriously concerned, the industry in 1922 formed the Motion Picture Producers and Distributors of America (MPPDA) in order to try to exert effective control over the films which it produced. The presidency was offered to Will H. Hays, federal Postmaster-General and well versed in politics. The object of the new organisation was to foster

> the common interests of those engaged in the motion picture industry in the United States, by establishing and maintaining the highest possible moral and artistic standards in motion picture production, by developing the educational as well as the entertainment value and the general usefulness of the motion picture, by diffusing accurate and reliable information with reference to the industry, by securing freedom from unjust or unlawful exactions, and by other lawful and proper means.[7]

One of Hays' first successes was his vigorous campaign against Massachusetts' pending censorship bill and in favour of self-regulation. After this, the only states to introduce film censorship provisions were Louisiana and Connecticut.

This was, of course, the 'Jazz Age', and what Hays called the 'licentious mood' of many of the books and plays which served as the raw material for the screen was a constant cause of concern. In order to deal with this problem he devised what came to be known as the 'Formula', whose preamble stated that, in their efforts 'to establish and maintain the highest possible moral and artistic standards of motion picture production', the members of the MPPDA were engaged in a special effort

> to prevent the prevalent type of book and play from becoming the prevalent type of picture; to exercise every possible care that only books and plays which are of the right type are used

for screen presentation; to avoid the picturization of books or plays which can be produced only after such changes as to leave the producer subject to a charge of deception; to avoid using titles which are indicative of a kind of picture which should not be produced, or by their suggestiveness seek to obtain attendance by deception, a thing equally reprehensible; and to prevent misleading, salacious or dishonest advertising.[8]

Members of the association undertook not to produce, distribute or exhibit any films which 'because of the unfit character, title, story, exploitation or picture itself' did not meet the requirements of the 'Formula', and all plays, novels and stories had to be submitted to the MPPDA before they were filmed. In the first year of the new system, sixty-seven projects were rejected, and by the time it was abandoned in 1930, 125 projects had failed to make it onto the screen.

The 'Formula' was administered by Colonel Jason Joy who, in order to facilitate contacts with producers, formed the Studio Relations Committee, which was in turn attached to the Association of Motion Picture Producers (AMPP). However, although initially the system was respected by producers, they soon began withholding material from the Committee, or simply ignored its recommendations (as in the case of *What Price Glory?* [1926] for example), and projects rejected by them such as *The Plastic Age* (1925), *The Constant Nymph* (1928) and *White Cargo* (1929) were filmed by companies which were not members of the MPPDA, although these could not be shown in cinemas controlled by MPPDA members.

'The don'ts and be carefuls'

Aware that any perceived weakness on the part of the MPPDA played straight into the hands of local censors or would-be censors, Hays drew up a list of those subjects which local and state censors were most likely to cut. As a result, in June 1927 the AMPP passed a resolution listing eleven things which 'shall not appear in pictures produced by members of this Association, irrespective of the manner in which they are treated', and twenty six others over which they should take care 'to the end that vulgarity and suggestiveness may be eliminated and that good taste may be emphasised'. These came to be known as the 'don'ts and be carefuls'. The former were:

1. Pointed profanity – by either title or lip – this includes the word 'God', 'Lord', 'Jesus', 'Christ' (unless used reverently in connection with proper religious ceremonies), 'hell', 'damn', 'Gawd', and every other profane and vulgar expression, however it may be spelled.
2. Any licentious or suggestive nudity – in fact or in silhouette; and any lecherous or licentious notice thereof by other characters in the picture.
3. The illegal traffic in drugs.
4. Any inference of sex perversion.
5. White slavery.
6. Miscegenation (sex relationships between black and white races).
7. Sex hygiene and venereal disease.
8. Scenes of actual childbirth – in fact or in silhouette.
9. Children's sex organs.
10. Ridicule of the clergy.
11. Wilful offence to any nation, race or creed.[9]

However, the old problem of the lack of any truly effective means of enforcing the rules stubbornly persisted. A familiar ruse, as Frank Miller points out, was that 'frequently, a film would depict an hour's worth of sinning, recorded in lavish detail, followed by a few minutes of speedy repentance before the final fade out'.[10] *Collier's* magazine dubbed the 'don'ts and be carefuls' as 'don't forget to stop before you have gone too far' and 'if you can't be good, be careful'. Meanwhile, the coming of sound had presented the Hays Office, as the Studio Relations Committee was now called with increasing frequency, with a whole series of new problems.

Since demands for more censorship at local and state levels were increasing, and since the press baron William Randolph Hearst was threatening to throw his newspaper empire behind the growing demands for federal censorship, Hays turned for help to Martin Quigley, who was both the publisher of the *Motion Picture Herald* and a devout and well-connected Catholic. Quigley had frequently editorialised against what he perceived as screen immorality, and, working with the Jesuit priest Father Daniel Lord of St Louis University, had developed a 'code to govern the making of talking, synchronised and silent motion pictures'. Hays presented this to the MPPDA board, which produced a document which would come to be known as the Production Code. Quigley himself served as a consultant to the committee. The Code was ratified unanimously by the Directors of the MPPDA on 31 March 1930.

The Production Code

In many ways a development of the 'don'ts and be carefuls', the Code began with a statement of general principles which stated that:

1. No picture shall be produced which will lower the standards of those who see it. Hence the sympathy of the audience shall never be thrown to the side of crime, wrongdoing, evil or sin.
2. Correct standards of life, subject only to the requirements of drama and entertainment, shall be presented.

3. Law, natural or human, shall not be ridiculed, nor shall sympathy be created for its violation.

More particularly, the Code incorporated all the 'don'ts' mentioned above and in addition required, among other things, that 'brutal killings are not to be presented in detail'; 'revenge in modern times shall not be justified'; 'the use of firearms should be restricted to essentials'; 'the use of liquor should never be excessively presented'; 'the sanctity of the institution of marriage and the home shall be upheld'; 'excessive and lustful kissing, lustful embraces, suggestive postures and gestures, are not to be shown'; 'passion should be so treated that these scenes do not stimulate the lower and baser elements'; 'sex perversion or any inference of it is forbidden'; 'the treatment of low, disgusting, unpleasant, though not necessarily evil, subjects should be subject always to the dictate of good taste and a regard for the sensibilities of the audience'; 'indecent or undue exposure is forbidden' and 'salacious, indecent, or obscene titles shall not be used'.[11]

But it is important to understand that the Code was more than simply a list of prohibitions and warnings. This becomes especially clear when one examines the less well-known section containing the reasons supporting the Code.[12] These reasons are worth exploring in more detail because they illuminate particularly clearly the kind of moral universe in which their authors believed that films should be taking place. Thus: 'Theatrical motion pictures, that is, pictures intended for the theatre as distinct from pictures intended for churches, schools, lecture halls, educational movements, social reform movements, etc., are primarily to be regarded as entertainment', which can be either helpful or harmful. The former 'tends to improve the race, or at least to re-create and rebuild human beings exhausted with the realities of life' and 'raises the whole standard of the nation', whilst the latter 'tends to degrade human beings, or to lower their standards of life and living' and 'lowers the whole living conditions and moral ideals of a race'. It is particularly important to regulate the cinema as a form of entertainment because 'no art has so quick and so widespread an appeal to the masses. It has become in an incredibly short period the art of the masses'. According to the Code, 'most arts appeal to the mature. This art appeals at once to every class', and because of the way in which films are distributed and exhibited, 'this art reaches places unpenetrated by other forms of art'. Consequently, 'it is difficult to produce films intended for only certain classes of people. The exhibitors' theatres are built for the masses, for the cultivated and the rude, the mature and the immature, the self-respecting and the criminal'. But the Code sees cinema as poten-tially dangerous not simply because it appeals to a working class audience but also because it is a *mass* medium, which is rather different: 'Psychologically, the larger the audience, the lower the moral mass resistance to suggestion'. But the cinema is also seen as a particularly dangerous form of art or entertainment because of its specific aesthetic qualities. Thus 'a book describes; a film vividly presents … the reaction of a reader to a book depends largely on the keenness of the reader's imagination; the reaction to a film depends on the vividness of presentation'. The audience for a film is brought closer to the story than the audience for a play through 'light, enlargement of character, presentation, scenic emphasis, etc.', but also, crucially, by 'the enthusiasm for and interest in the film actors and actresses', which 'makes the audience largely sympathetic toward the characters they portray and the stories in which they figure. Hence the audience is more ready to confuse actor and actress and the characters they portray, and it is most receptive of the emotions and ideals presented by their favourite stars'. In more general terms, 'the mobility, popularity, accessibility, emotional appeal, vividness, straightforward presentation of fact in the film make far more contact with a larger audience and for greater emotional appeal. Hence the larger moral responsibilities of the motion pictures'.

In discussing these responsibilities, the Code enlarges on both the general principles and particular applications outlined above. Thus, for example, regarding the requirement that 'the sympathy of the audience shall never be thrown to the side of crime, wrongdoing, evil or sin', the Code notes that:

> Sympathy with a person who sins is not the same thing as sympathy with the sin or crime of which he is guilty. We may feel sorry for the plight of the murderer or even understand the circumstances which led him to his crime. We may not feel sympathy with the wrong which he has done. The presentation of evil is often essential for art or fiction or drama. This in itself is not wrong provided:
> a. That evil is not presented alluringly. Even if later in the film the evil is condemned or punished, it must not be allowed to appear so attractive that the audience's emotions are drawn to desire or approve so strongly that later the condemnation is forgotten and only the apparent joy of the sin remembered.
> b. That throughout, the audience feels sure that evil is wrong and good is right.

To this end, the Code erects a distinction between 'sin which repels by its very nature, and sins which often attract'. In the first category come murder, most theft, lying, cruelty and so on, which are 'naturally unattractive. The audience instinctively condemns all such and is repelled'. What needs to be avoided here, however, is the 'hardening of the audience, especially of those who are young and impressionable, to the thought and fact of crime. People can become accustomed even to murder, cruelty, brutality, and repellent crimes, if these are too frequently repeated'. Even more care needs to be taken when dealing with 'sex sins, sins and crimes of apparent heroism, such as banditry, daring thefts, leadership in evil, organised crime, revenge, etc.'. Inevitably, 'sex sins' loom particularly large here. Thus the Code states:

> In the case of impure love, the love which society has always regarded as wrong, and which has been banned by divine law, the following are important:
> 1. Impure love must not be presented as attractive and beautiful.
> 2. It must not be the subject of comedy or farce, or treated as material for laughter.
> 3. It must not be presented in such a way as to arouse passion or morbid curiosity on the part of the audience.
> 4. It must not be made to seem right and permissible.
> 5. In general, it must not be detailed in method and manner.

Although the new Code was stricter and far more elaborate than any previous measures introduced by the film industry, it did not bring about any major changes in the way in which the Studio Relations Committee worked. Every film had to be submitted to them before being sent to the laboratories for printing. If it was felt that the film violated the Code, the producer was not allowed to release the print until the required changes had been made. Script submission was made compulsory in October 1931.

But still the problem of enforcing the Code's provisions remained, and many of the industry's critics felt that the Hays Office was far too liberal in its judgements. Crime films were the object of considerable controversy in the early 1930s, with works such as *Little Caesar* (1931), *The Public Enemy* (1931) and *Scarface* (1932) being accused of making criminals too attractive and suggesting that crime pays. But the major cause of criticism was, inevitably, sex. Adaptations of Theodore Dreiser's *An American Tragedy* (1931) and Ferenc Molnár's *The Guardsman* (1931), both previously banned by the Committee, finally made it to the screen. Marlene Dietrich was accused of glorifying adultery in *The Scarlet Empress* (1934); *Dr Jekyll and Mr Hyde* (1931) mingled sex and horror; Cecil B. De Mille's biblical epic *The Sign of the Cross* (1932) made the very most of the decadence of ancient Rome; Busby Berkeley's famous musicals showed as much female flesh as they could get away with, and stars such as Jean Harlow in *Red-Headed Woman* (1932) and *Red Dust* (1932), and Mae West in *She Done Him Wrong* (1933) and *I'm No Angel* (1933) were as hated by some (not least the Hearst press) as they were loved by others.

The problem for Hollywood was that whilst many of these controversial films drove the censorious into a frenzy, ran into censorship problems where local or state-level boards existed, and fed demands for censorship at the federal level, they were also extremely popular and thus highly profitable. Clearly this situation could not continue indefinitely, and in 1933 two things happened which were finally to give the Code the teeth which it had hitherto lacked.

First came the publication of the Payne Fund studies, which purported to show that films exercise a highly negative influence on children and young people. These originated from a grant given in 1929 to the pro-censorship group the Motion Picture Research Council by the Payne Study and Experiment Fund to analyse the influence of film on behaviour. The first results of their research appeared in the January 1933 issue of *McCall's* magazine, to considerable and widespread public consternation, which was only further intensified when the Council hired the writer Henry James Forman to popularise its findings in the book *Our Movie Made Children*, which became a best-seller. According to Forman: 'Fagin's school was child's play to this curriculum of crime', and 'the road to delinquency, in a few words, is heavily dotted with movie addicts, and obviously, it needs no crusaders or preachers or reformers to come to this conclusion'.[13] No matter that some of those involved in the original research claimed that Payne had misrepresented their findings, and that others raised serious doubts about the methodology used in that research, the whole episode did a great deal to reinforce the notion, already prevalent in certain quarters, that the movies were a force for the bad.

By this time, even Hollywood was feeling the effects of the Depression, and this made it more vulnerable to attack and criticism, especially if this resulted in fewer people going to the cinema. And it was precisely at this point that the Catholic Church decided to strike.

During the summer of 1933, an increasing number of churchmen had spoken out against the film industry. For example, in a speech to the National Conference of Catholic Charities in New York, Archbishop Cicognani had proclaimed: 'What a massacre of innocent youth is taking place hour by hour! How shall the crimes that have their direct source in motion pictures be measured?'[14] This activity reached its climax in November 1933 when the Catholic bishops at their annual Synod formed a special committee to look into the situation. By the following April, this had become the Legion of Decency, which both campaigned for what it regarded as better films and organised boycotts of those it deemed offensive. On applying to join, members took a pledge, which stated that:

> I wish to join the Legion of Decency, which condemns vile and unwholesome moving pictures. I unite with all who protest against them as a grave menace to youth, to home life, to country and to religion. I condemn absolutely those salacious motion pictures which, with other degrading agencies, are corrupting public morals and promoting a sex mania in our

land ... I make this protest in a spirit of self-respect, and with
the conviction that the American public does not demand filthy
pictures, but clean entertainment and educational features.[15]

In May 1934, the Detroit branch of the Legion issued a list of
sixty-three films which it condemned, forty-three of which had
been passed by the Studio Relations Committee. At about the
same time, Father Daniel Lord began to name five condemned
films each month in his magazine *Queen's Work*. The first
boycott organised by the Legion took place in Philadelphia: box
office takings fell by forty per cent. The Federal Council of
Churches of Christ in America was threatening to enlist all of its
twenty-two million members in the Legion and to campaign for
federal censorship as well. The work of the Legion also began to
attract support from the Protestant and Jewish communities.
Matters were reaching crisis point for Hollywood.

The Production Code Administration

Colonel Joy had left the Hays Office in 1932 to be replaced
briefly by James Wingate. He in turn had been succeeded by
Joseph Breen, another Catholic, who now undertook to force
the studios to obey the Code. Indeed, some sources suggest that
Breen and Martin Quigley actually encouraged the Church to
embark on its campaign against the movies as a way of bringing
the studios finally into line. But whatever the case, the Catholic
bishops agreed to relax the campaign if the Code was properly
enforced. Thus on 1 July 1934, the Studio Relations Committee
became the Production Code Administration (PCA), headed by
Breen and with an expanded staff. A new seal of approval was
created, which was signed by the Director of the PCA, and no
member company of the MPPDA was allowed to distribute or
exhibit any film which had not been awarded this seal. Every

print of every film passed by the PCA had to bear the seal. Members who failed to comply with the Code's provisions could be fined $25,000.

Just how rigorous was this new system is described by Raymond Moley in his 1947 book *The Hays Office*, in which he lays out the major stages of the approval process through which any film submitted to the PCA had to pass:

1. A preliminary conference between Breen or other members of the staff of the PCA and the producer, to consider the basic story before the screen adaptation is written or purchased; at this point the plot as a whole is discussed in its relation to the Code.
2. Careful scrutiny of the script submitted by the producing company.
3. Scenario conferences with writers and others to effect necessary changes in the script.
4. Approval in writing by Breen of the script for production.
5. Continued conferences during production, so that any changes made in the script as well as all lyrics, costumes and sets may be observed and passed upon.
6. Preview of separate sequences during the course of production, whenever the producer is in doubt about their conformity with the Code; this is done upon the request of the producer.
7. Preview of the completed picture in the PCA viewing theatre by the same two staff members who worked on the script and by a third staff member who comes to the picture with a fresh mind.
8. After deletion of scenes, dialogue, etc. which violate the Code, issue of its certificate of approval by the Production Code Administration.[16]

This system was to stay in place until 1968, and although many film-makers tried to get away with as much as they could, was to prove remarkably effective until the mid-1950s. One of Breen's first acts was to demand the re-editing or withdrawal of a number of films already in circulation. Into the former category fell *She Done Him Wrong*, *I'm No Angel*, *The Story of Temple Drake* (a 1933 adaptation of William Faulkner's *Sanctuary*), the 1934 revue *George White's Scandals* (in which Alice Fay's song 'Oh You Nasty Man' and the number 'Your Dog Loves My Dog' had proved particularly problematic), and the Barbara Stanwyck vehicle *Baby Face* (1933). Breen refused to re-release *Design for Living* (directed in 1933 by Ernst Lubitsch from the play by Noel Coward), the Marlene Dietrich vehicles *The Song of Songs* (1933) and *The Blue Angel* (1930), and *Scarface*. *Little Caesar* and *The Public Enemy* remained banned until 1953. Cuts had to be made in *King Kong* (1933), *All Quiet on the Western Front* (1930) and *A Farewell to Arms* (1932) before they could be re-released.

When it came to new films, the situation was clearly different. As we have seen, the PCA was involved at every stage of the production of a film, and works were shaped as they went along so as to fit in with the Code's requirements. Inevitably this involved a great deal of self-censorship. For example, before the Greta Garbo vehicles *Camille* (1936) and *Anna Karenina* (1935) could be filmed, their sources, Alexandre Dumas *fils' La Dame aux Camélias* and Tolstoy's novel respectively, had to be very considerably re-jigged in order to satisfy Breen that they did not glorify or justify adultery. And any hint of lesbianism had to be removed from the screen adaptation of Lillian Hellman's play *The Children's Hour*, which was filmed in 1936 as *These Three*.

Bans were imposed on proposed projects, not on finished films, simply because works which would have been taboo never got as far as being produced in the first place. However, because a completed film sometimes came across as in some way different from the script which had been submitted prior to production, cutting was not uncommon. Inevitably, in the early days of the new order Mae West's latest releases came in for particular scrutiny, and *Belle of the Nineties* (1934), *Klondike Annie* (1936) and *Every Day's a Holiday* (1937) suffered cuts before they could be released. Indeed, the taming of Mae West in her post-1934 pictures contributed considerably to her declining popularity.

However, the outbreak of the Second World War brought problems for the PCA. With American profits frozen in Britain, and American films banned in Germany and the occupied territories, Hollywood looked to increased profits from the home box office, and sought clearance for controversial properties such as *Tobacco Road* (1941) and *Kings's Row* (1942). On 29 March 1941, Breen wrote to Hays: 'In recent months we have noted a marked tendency on the part of studios to more and more undrape women's breasts. In recent weeks the practice has become so prevalent as to make it necessary for us, almost every day, to hold up a picture'.[17] In 1941 the Legion of Decency, for the first time since 1934, condemned a film which had been given a seal: this was the Garbo vehicle *Two-Faced Woman* (1941), which the Legion felt displayed an 'immoral and un-Christian attitude to marriage and its obligations; impudently suggestive scenes, dialogue and situations; suggestive costumes'. Archbishop Francis Spellman denounced it in a letter read from the pulpits of all New York churches; New York congressman Martin Kennedy called the film 'an affront to the Congress of the United States'; and the Legion's secretary, the Reverend John McClafferty, warned Hollywood 'not to let the wartime trend "away from God" creep into movies'.[18]

This last remark points towards the wider social factors which would lead film-makers to push the PCA into accepting more adult fare during the war years. Thanks to wartime employment, people, and especially young people, had more money to spend on entertainment. The phenomenon of the teenager had begun to develop. The deaths of hundreds of thousands of American servicemen encouraged people to live for the moment. Alcohol consumption, juvenile crime and divorce all increased substantially. Thus during and just after the war the PCA passed (albeit with alterations) such hitherto unthinkable films as *Double Indemnity* (1944), *The Big Sleep* (1946), *Forever Amber* (1947), *Duel in the Sun* (1946), and even *The Postman Always Rings Twice* (1946), proposals for which had been turned down flat in 1933 and 1934. The war had unleashed forces which Hollywood could not ignore.

'A significant medium for the communication of ideas'

In 1948, in *United States v. Paramount Pictures*, the control by the major studios over production, distribution and exhibition was found to violate anti-trust laws. The studios were thus forced to sell their cinemas, which in turn meant that independent producers now had access to the major cinema chains, which could, in theory at least, show films without the PCA seal. One of the first beneficiaries of this was the 1948 Italian neo-realist film *Ladri di biciclette* (known as *Bicycle Thieves* in the UK and *The Bicycle Thief* in the US), which Breen turned down on account of a shot in which a young boy is about to relieve himself in the street, and another in which he and his father mistakenly enter a brothel. The National Council on Freedom from Censorship described this as 'a shocking demonstration of censorship' and a 'violation of free thought and expression, and a disgrace to the industry' whilst the *New York Times* critic Bosley Crowther alleged that the PCA staff had 'put their minds in deep freeze', and voiced the feelings of many in Hollywood when he argued that the ban constituted 'the sort of resistance to liberalisation or change that widely and perilously oppresses the whole industry today'.[19] However, by mid-April 1950 the film was playing in forty-six independent cinemas, and, sensing that they were missing out on a valuable commercial opportunity, three of the major cinema chains announced that they too would be booking it. This was a major blow to the system of Code compliance.

Another Italian film was the subject of an important legal ruling in 1952. This was Roberto Rossellini's *Il Miracolo* (*The Miracle*), which was in fact a segment from the 1948 episode film *L'Amore* (*Ways of Love*). The story of a young peasant woman who believes that she is pregnant with the Son of God, it was seen by many Catholics as a satire on the virgin birth. Though passed by the New York censorship board, it was condemned by the Legion of Decency when it opened at the Paris Theatre on 12 December 1950. On 15 February 1951, the New York Board of Regents, which supervised the censorship board, revoked the film's licence on the grounds that the film was sacrilegious and violated the religious freedom of Christians. The distributor, Joseph Burstyn, challenged the ban, but it was upheld by the New York State Supreme Court, which cited the precedent set by the Ohio case in 1915. Burstyn then appealed to the US Supreme Court, which in May 1952, handed down a landmark ruling which went a long way to overturning the Ohio one:

> It cannot be doubted that motion pictures are a significant medium for the communication of ideas. They may affect public attitudes and behaviour in a variety of ways, ranging from direct espousal of a political or social doctrine to the subtle shaping of thought which characterises all artistic expression. The importance of motion pictures as an organ of public opinion is not lessened by the fact that they are designed to entertain as well as to inform.
>
> Nor should film be subject to censorship because it is an industry conducted for profit, as such a category would also include the press. Finally, the medium's supposed capacity for

evil, if it existed at all, was not sufficient justification for substantially unbridled censorship such as we have here.[20]

Although this judgement did not actually rule that film censorship was unconstitutional, it did lead to a series of further cases in which the Supreme Court overturned the decisions of local or state censors. State censorship came to an end in Ohio in 1954, Massachusetts in 1955 and Pennsylvania in 1956.

Liberalisation of the enforcement of the PCA Code was still a slow process, however. Thus Elia Kazan's 1951 adaptation of Tennessee Williams' *A Streetcar Named Desire* had to be considerably toned down, even though the PCA admitted that for the first time it had passed a film which was clearly not family entertainment; the same year William Wyler's *Detective Story* lost any reference to abortion, and in 1953 it proved impossible for Fred Zinnemann to bring to the screen James Jones' novel *From Here to Eternity* without considerable revisions. On the other hand, even though shorn of some of their more controversial elements, these films did show that, within limits, the PCA was prepared to let Hollywood tackle more adult themes. And this was particularly necessary now that television was eating into the family audience. This may have been one of the reasons why, when the PCA refused to grant a seal to Otto Preminger's 1953 sex comedy *The Moon is Blue*, United Artists (which was not a member of the MPAA) decided to distribute it anyway. Although condemned by the Legion of Decency – or maybe partly because of this – the film did extremely good business, running in three major cinema chains, and making it to fifteenth in *Variety*'s top fifty for 1953.

Taboo busting

In February 1954 Joseph Breen announced that he was retiring from the PCA, and his place was taken by his chief assistant Geoffrey Shurlock, who was a Protestant, the following

October. Rather more flexible and pragmatic than his predeces-
sor, he nonetheless in 1956 refused a seal to *The Man with the
Golden Arm*, Preminger's film about drug addiction starring
Frank Sinatra. United Artists again distributed it successfully
without a seal, and it was not condemned by the Legion, which
was beginning to become a little more liberal in its judgements.
As a consequence the Code was revised to allow the responsible
depiction of drug addiction, prostitution, childbirth and sexual
relations between different ethnic groups. The words 'hell' and
'damn' were also permitted. The only remaining taboos were
nudity, sexual perversion and venereal disease. From now on,
the treatment of a subject would be far more important than the
mere subject itself. This may explain why Stanley Kubrick's
1962 film of *Lolita* was passed with few cuts, although in his
screenplay the author of the original novel, Vladimir Nabokov,
had made it more acceptable to the PCA, not least by increasing
Lolita's age from twelve to fifteen. Explicit references to
homosexuality were still excised from Vincente Minnelli's *Tea
and Sympathy* (1956), and from two Tennessee Williams
adaptations, *Cat on a Hot Tin Roof* (1958) and *Suddenly Last
Summer* (1959), but in 1961 *The Children's Hour* (based on the
play by Lillian Hellman mentioned above) finally broke that
particular taboo, followed the next year by Otto Preminger's
Advise and Consent. On 3 October 1961, the Code was amended
to read: 'In keeping with the culture, the mores and the values
of our time, homosexuality and other sexual aberrations may
now be treated with care, discretion and restraint'.[21]

The final taboo to be broken was nudity, and this occurred
with Sidney Lumet's *The Pawnbroker* (1964). Nudity had long
been staple fare of the low-budget, independent movies shown
in the grindhouses, but had been cut out of those few
mainstream US feature films which attempted it, such as
Splendour in the Grass (1961), *Of Human Bondage* (1964) and *The
Carpetbaggers* (1964). There were only two brief scenes of nudity

in *The Pawnbroker*, which the PCA originally refused to pass. However, the producers appealed to the Production Code Review Board, and the film was granted 'special exemption' provided the scenes were slightly shortened. It was, however, condemned by the Legion, but they were clearly divided over the film, and many Catholics actually defended it. In 1966 the increasingly liberal and diverse Legion changed its name to the National Catholic Office of Motion Pictures.

The language barrier was finally broken by the 1966 film version of Edward Albee's 1962 play *Who's Afraid of Virginia Woolf?*. This was rejected by Shurlock, and again the Review Board was asked to step in. By this time, its producers (Warner Bros.) had made it clear that, if passed, it would be shown only to those over eighteen. The Board thus granted this film too a 'special exemption', requesting only the deletion of the words 'frigging' and 'screw you', and this met with the approval of the new Catholic office

In May 1966 Jack Valenti had taken over as president of the MPAA, and it was clear to him, as to many others in the industry, that the old Production Code system was simply no longer workable in a society undergoing such rapid change as the US. One possibility was to revise the Code, but when this was done in September 1966, it was almost immediately detonated by the importation of Antonioni's *Blow-Up* (1966). Refused a seal and condemned by the Catholics, the film was released by MGM through a subsidiary, Premier Films, and made almost $7 million in its first six months. The new Code also allowed for certain films to be classed as 'suggested for mature audiences', but this simply gave film-makers more leeway to explore adult themes.

The Code and Rating Administration

The other alternative was to introduce an age classification system, which is anyway what in effect had come into existence with *Who's Afraid of Virginia Woolf?* – almost certainly with the active collaboration of the Catholic Church, which by this time supported the creation of just such a system. And although there were many in the industry who feared that classification would lower box office revenues on certain titles, just such a system was announced on 7 October 1968. Its preamble stated:

> This Code is designed to keep in close harmony with the mores, culture, the moral sense and change in our society. The objectives of the Code are:
> 1. To encourage artistic expression by expanding creative freedom.
> 2. To assure that the freedom which encourages the artist remains responsible and sensitive to the standards of the larger society.[22]

The Code itself, which would be run by the Code and Rating Administration (CARA), consisted of four ratings: G, suggested for general audiences; M, suggested for mature audiences – adults and mature young people; R, restricted – persons under sixteen not admitted unless accompanied by parent or adult guardian; and X – persons under sixteen not admitted. The main reason for including this last category was that the Supreme Court had recently ruled, in *Ginsberg v. New York*, that it was legal to protect young people (but not adults) from pornography, and in *Interstate Circuit v. Dallas* that the Constitution permitted local censorship boards to ban under-sixteens from seeing certain films. But unlike the other ratings, the X was not copyrighted, as it was intended that any film-maker who saw no point in submitting their film to CARA could simply impose an X rating upon it themselves. Valenti was also keen that the major studios did not become associated with pornographic movies. However, the X and its 1990 replacement, the NC-17, were to become a source of considerable controversy and, some would argue, of censorship in the years that followed.

In 1969, United Artists decided to self-impose an X on *Midnight Cowboy*, which went on to become the only X-rated film to win an Oscar for best picture. The following year, the X-rated *A Clockwork Orange* won the New York Film Critics Award for best picture of 1970. Partly as a result, CARA raised the age restriction on R from sixteen to seventeen in 1970, allowing films such as *Women in Love* (1969), *Fellini-Satyricon* (1969), *M*A*S*H* (1970), and *Zabriskie Point* (1970) to be awarded an R. However, not least because producers of far less reputable pictures were awarding their films Xs, and indeed XXs and XXXs, precisely in order to signal their high-octane content, the X rapidly acquired a stigma, and in particular the stigma of pornography. Very rapidly, half the cinemas in America refused to show X-rated films, and about thirty big city newspapers, along with many radio and TV stations, refused to advertise them. A film awarded an X could thus face the loss of at least half of its potential box-office receipts. Later, video chains such as Blockbuster would refuse to carry films awarded an NC-17 (the successor to the X). Matters were not helped by Dr Jacqueline Bouhoutsos, a child psychologist working for CARA, calling X films 'garbage, pictures that shouldn't have been made for anybody, films without any kind of artistic merit, poor taste, disgusting, repulsive'[23] Consequently, producers submitted to cuts in order to avoid these ratings, and the number of films rated X by CARA began to decline soon after the category's inception. *The French Connection* (1971) was cut at script stage, and *If* (1968) and *Straw Dogs* (1971) were cut for their US releases. In 1991, Oliver Stone's *Natural Born Killers* was considerably cut in order to receive an R, and Harvey Weinstein of the distributors Miramax called the NC-17 'economic suicide'. At the same time, however, the system has been accused of favouring movies produced by big studios and disadvantaging those made by independents – *The Exorcist* (1973) escaping with an R being a case in point. It is argued that the majors are able to exercise more clout when it comes to appeals, and can more easily afford to re-edit films or release them in different versions

Whether or not film classification as practiced by the MPAA is a form of censorship is a matter of considerable debate. On the one hand, there is no law requiring film-makers to submit their works to the MPAA. Equally, cinema owners are perfectly within their rights not to show films of which they disapprove. As Jack Valenti himself put it: 'If film-makers have a right to tell a story, and no one can force them to censor that work, then exhibitors have a concomitant right to be able to choose what material they want to exhibit in their theatres … Some theatre owners are in a shopping mall, they're in a neighbourhood. There are certain kinds of pictures they don't want to play'.[24] On the other hand, writers and directors working for MPAA members frequently have to engage in various forms of self-censorship if they want to see their work on the screen, and this effectively renders the MPAA scheme a form of censorship rather than simply an exercise in editorial judgement or consumer guidance. In this respect it's significant that when the distributors Miramax challenged the X given to Pedro Almodovar's *Tie Me Up, Tie Me Down* (1990), the judge in the case called the MPAA system 'an effective form of censorship' because 'films are produced and *negotiated* to fit the ratings', and thus, 'contrary to our jurisprudence, which protects all forms of expression, the rating system censors serious films by the force of economic pressure'.[25]

We shall return at some length in chapter 5 to considering economic forces as agents of censorship.

4
Councillors and classifiers

As in the United States, the coming of the cinema in Britain was greeted with a great deal of apprehension by the censorious, and, again, it was the fact that it was a popular art form, one that appealed particularly to working class audiences, that was of particular concern. Here, too, it was the creation of various forms of local censorship bodies, and the threat of central government censorship, that spurred the industry into devising its own system of censorship, which is run by the British Board of Film Classification (BBFC, originally Censors). The British system, however, has closer links with the state, at both a local and national level, than does the American one.

'An official point of view'

The BBFC's founding, and its continued existence, have to be understood primarily as a response to local councils' powers of film censorship. The 1909 Cinematograph Act gave local authorities power to impose conditions on film exhibition in order to protect the public against fire hazards, but councils soon began to abuse these licensing powers by withholding licences from cinemas which showed films which the authorities deemed unsuitable. And so, in 1912, the Cinematograph Exhibitors' Association, faced with an increasingly bewildering array of varying local censorship practices and standards, decided to form the British Board of Film Censors, described by the *Bioscope* on

21 November 1912 as 'a purely independent and impartial body, whose duty it will be to induce confidence in the minds of the licensing authorities, and of those who have in their charge the moral welfare of the community generally'.[1] Its first President was George Alexander Redford, who appointed four examiners to work with him, and the Board issued two types of certificate: U (Universal) and A (Public, which gradually came to be seen as indicating that a film was more suitable for adult audiences). Significantly, Redford was previously an Examiner for the Lord Chamberlain, in which role he had banned Shaw's *Mrs Warren's Profession* and Harley Granville-Barker's *Waste*, and who, as we saw in chapter 2, p. 41, defined that role as 'simply bringing to bear an official point of view and keeping up a standard'. Nothing, in fact, could more succinctly define the role of the BBFC for many decades to come.

In 1916, agitation from the police, who had convinced themselves that a rise in juvenile crime was entirely the fault of the cinema, led the government to propose the creation of a Central Board of Censorship under the authority of the Home Office. Because of a change of government nothing finally came of this very real threat, but it, and the continued activities of the local councils, served to remind the film industry that it needed to respect the decisions of the BBFC. In 1924 the Board received judicial recognition when the Divisional Court upheld the validity of a condition that: 'no cinematograph film ... which has not been passed for ... exhibition by the BBFC shall be exhibited without the express consent of the council'.[2] This effectively meant that as long as a local council reserved the right to overrule BBFC decisions when it disagreed with them, it was entitled to make it a condition of granting a licence to a cinema that that cinema screened only films passed by the BBFC. This position was later upheld by the Court of Appeal in 1976 when Lord Denning said that: 'I do not think the county councils can delegate the whole of their responsibilities to the board, but they can treat the board as an advisory body whose views they can accept or reject; provided that the final decision – aye or nay – rests with the county council'.[3]

The licensing powers of local authorities, and thus their effective ability to act as film censors, of course survived the passing of flammable film. In 1952, Section 3 of the Cinematograph Act imposed a duty on licensing authorities to restrict the admission of children to cinemas that showed works 'designated by the licensing authority or such other body as may be specified in the licence, as works unsuitable for children', and this reference to "such other body" was the first parliamentary acknowledgement of the BBFC. Thus the Act established the Board's position, if not as a censorship body, then at least as an authorised classifier of films unsuitable for young people.

In 1979 the Williams Committee on Obscenity and Film Censorship castigated this form of local censorship as a duplication of the activities of the BBFC and of the function of the Obscene Publications Act. It was also clear that they thought the whole thing a waste of local councillors' time and of ratepayers' money. However, the liberalising recommendations of this official enquiry were studiously ignored by the incoming Tory government, and have been ignored ever since. Indeed, local authorities' licensing provisions were re-enacted in 1982 and consolidated in the 1985 Cinemas Act. Most local authorities now adopt the following 'model licensing conditions' drafted by the Home Office:

(a) No film, other than a current newsreel, shall be exhibited unless it has received a certificate of the British Board of Film Classification or is the subject of the licensing authority's permission;

(b) no young people shall be admitted to any exhibition of a film classified by the Board as unsuitable for them, unless with the local authority's permission;

(c) no film shall be exhibited if the licensing authority gives notice in writing prohibiting its exhibition on the ground that it 'would offend against good taste or decency or would be likely to encourage or incite to crime or to lead to disorder or to be offensive to public feeling';

(d) the nature of the certificate given to any film shall be indicated in any advertising for the film, at the cinema entrance (together with an explanation of its effect), and on the screen immediately before the film is shown;

(e) displays outside the cinema shall not depict any scene or incident not in the film as approved.[4]

And so, since, in the last analysis, the BBFC has to take into account, when classifying a film, the sensibilities of local fire brigade or watch committees, this means, as Geoffrey Robertson states, that in Britain: 'The cinema, alone of art forms, is subject to moral judgement by local councils' (1993: 263).[5] This is a situation highly unlikely to change. Films banned by numerous local councils have included, *Ulysses* (1967), *The Devils* (1971), *Straw Dogs* (1971), *Last Tango in Paris* (1972) and *The Life of Brian* (1979).

Systemic links

However, this is by no means the limit of the BBFC's relationship with the state. Until the Video Recordings Act 1984 gave statutory force to the BBFC's video certificates (see below), it was generally regarded as a private, industry body, and this was certainly the image which both the Board and successive governments were at pains to promote. However, this has served simply to obscure and mystify the BBFC's systemic links with the state. In this respect, the backgrounds of the earlier presidents are particularly instructive. For example, Redford's successor in 1916, T.P. O'Connor had been not only an MP but a very senior one, being 'father' of the House of Commons. He was succeeded in 1929 by Sir Edward Shortt, a former Chief Secretary for Ireland and Home Secretary; in the former role he had acquired a reputation as an expert on counter-subversion, and in the latter he had had to deal with labour agitation in the shipyards on the banks of the Clyde in Scotland, police strikes, and disaffection and mutiny in the army. Shortt's successor, Lord Tyrell, was a former Permanent Head of the Foreign Office, where previously he had founded the News Department and headed the Political Intelligence Department. Furthermore, Joseph Brooke-Wilkinson, the Secretary of the Board from 1913 to 1949, had been in charge of British film propaganda to neutral nations during the First World War, and was also a member of the secret CID Committee on Censorship. In other words these were men of extremely high political position with impeccable contacts: the Establishment personified. Indeed, of the four examiners at work in 1939, three had high-ranking military backgrounds. Even after the Second World War, this tradition continued. Thus Sir Sidney West Harris, who was appointed in 1947, had been an Assistant Under-Secretary at the Home Office. As Nicholas Pronay puts it, the presence of men such as Tyrell and Short at the head of the BBFC in its early years proves

> the existence of high-level contacts, of wide experience of politics and government at the highest level, and of knowledge about other operations being conducted in the field of propaganda and counter-propaganda, which are the essential perquisites for conducting political censorship. They also reveal the top-quality minds, political finesse and personal authority without which an operation requiring as great an intelligence and sophistication as the conduct of political censorship in a country such as Britain could not survive for a moment.[6]

The President of the BBFC thus did not for one moment need to be told what to do by government; as Pronay argues, his whole 'experience and background ensured that he could be relied upon to know what was needed ... It made no difference to his "official" standing either where the money for his salary came from or what position, if any, the organisation formally possessed.[7] The pre-video era BBFC was thus a private body, financed by the fees charged for classifying and cutting films and not by taxpayers' money, with its president 'elected' by the industry's own trade association. As such the BBFC did not fall within the definition of a state organisation, was free from public scrutiny and obligation, and allowed the Home Secretary to wash his hands in Parliament of the responsibility for cutting, banning or passing any particular film. As the Home Secretary Herbert Morrison put in 1942:

> I freely admit that this is a curious arrangement, but the British have a very great habit of making curious arrangements that work very well, and this works. Frankly, I do not wish to be the Minister who has to answer questions in the House as to whether particular films should or should not be censored. I think it would be dangerous for the Home Secretary to have direct powers himself in this matter.[8]

However, what this rather self-satisfied formulation ignores is the very considerable *indirect* powers exercised by the Home Secretary over film censorship, and the odd fact that there was only ever one candidate for BBFC President, who 'emerged' mysteriously only after consultation with, and with the approval of, the Home Secretary. Nor did this situation change after the Second World War. In 1952 a PEP report stated that: 'The practice is to elect a man, usually prominent in public life, who is acceptable to a Trade Committee as well as to the Home Secretary and the licensing authorities', whilst the then BBFC Secretary John Trevelyan noted in 1963 that the President 'is appointed by a joint committee representative of all branches of the film industry, after informal consultation with the Home Secretary and the principal local authority associations'.[9]

Champion of the established order

There should not be the slightest doubt that the censorship exercised by the BBFC in the years preceding the Second World War was political in every sense of the word, and far more so than that exercised by the PCA in the United States. In 1917 the Board's President T.P. O'Connor presented to the National Council of Public Morals a list of forty-three rules which the BBFC had been using since its inception. These included bans on 'references to controversial politics', 'relations of Capital and Labour', 'realistic horrors of warfare', 'incidents having a tendency to disparage our allies' and 'subjects dealing with India, in which British officers are seen in an odious light, and otherwise attempting to suggest the disloyalty of Native States, or bringing into disrepute British prestige in the Empire'.[10] It could perhaps be argued that some of these rules might have been defensible in wartime, but by 1919 the grounds for cutting films appear to have expanded to sixty-seven, although admittedly most of the new ones related to social mores, of which the BBFC was a fierce guardian. The BBFC annual report for 1919 clearly shows that the Board saw itself as the champion of the established order in every area of life, explaining that examiners are

> guided by the main broad principles that nothing should be passed which is calculated to demoralise an audience, that can teach the methods of, or extenuate, crime, that can undermine the teachings of morality, that tends to bring the institution of marriage into contempt, or lower the sacredness of family ties.

> Objection is taken to incidents which bring Public Characters into contempt, when acting in their capacity as such, together with subjects which might wound the susceptibilities of foreign peoples. The question of religious observances is very carefully considered, also subjects which are calculated to foment violent social unrest.[11]

In order fully to understand the import of this last stipulation, it needs to be borne in mind that many people were living in daily terror of working class militancy in Britain; this was as a result of the success of the Russian revolution, the narrow failure of the revolution in Germany, the increased representation of Labour at Westminster, and industrial unrest in various parts of the country. Inevitably, then, the great Soviet classics of Eisenstein, Pudovkin and Vertov were entirely taboo for general audiences, but the fact that they were allowed to be shown to members of the Film Society furnishes ample proof, if any were needed, of the major role which considerations of class played in the operations of the BBFC at this time.

That the Board was regularly in consultation with government, and was indeed proud of the fact, is clear from its 1921 report which states that:

> Films are now and then submitted to the Board which raise important questions of public policy and public interest. The Board has always held itself free to ask for expert information when the need arises – sometimes it is from public departments, sometimes from men representative of social or religious opinion. The consultation of public authorities is very useful and indeed essential when films deal with subjects that touch racial or national interests, the history and personalities of great historical events, the existence and the expediency and measure of their exhibition. While, of course, reserving their final and independent judgement, the Board must offer its gratitude for

the willingness and the readiness with which the heads and officials of all these public departments have given their time and experience to the guidance of the Board. On the other hand, consultation of men representative of social and religious opinion is an additional safeguard against the admission to the film of any of the controversial themes and incidents that are in opposition to the film being used as an agent for violent controversy in social or public life.[12]

The 1926 report lists seventy-three grounds on which films were cut that year, new ones including 'inflammatory sub-titles and Bolshevist Propaganda', 'equivocal situations between white girls and men of other races', and 'incidents which reflect a mistaken conception of the Police Forces in this country in the administration of justice'.[13] After 1931 these annual reports ceased, but added to the list of prohibitions in that decade were 'references to H.R.H. the Prince of Wales', 'references to Royal Personages at home and abroad' (both of these clearly designed to keep off the screen any reference to the future king's affair with Mrs Simpson), 'British possessions represented as lawless sinks of depravity', and 'reflection on wife of responsible British official stationed in the East'.[14]

Appeasement

Just how overtly political was the censorship carried out by the BBFC before the Second World War can be judged by the fate of works dealing with Nazi Germany, during the 1930s regarded as a friendly nation and one which the British government did its utmost to appease. In 1933 two Gaumont-British proposals, *A German Tragedy* and *City Without Jews*, were turned down, as was the screenplay *The Mad Dog of Europe* in 1934. The same year the documentary *Hitler's Reign of Terror* was banned, as was Adrian Brunel and Ivor Montagu's *Free Thälmann* in 1935. The following year the Board turned down a proposal to remake Robert Wiene's silent German classic *The Cabinet of Dr Caligari*; the BBFC had heavily cut the 1920 original (on grounds of taste), and amongst the items in the proposed remake to which it took exception was a comic waxwork of Hitler. By 1938 the BBFC was interfering with the US newsreel *The March of Time*, and banned outright its special issue *Inside Nazi Germany* on the grounds that 'it would give offence to a nation with whom we are on terms of friendship and which it would be impolitic to offend'. By this time, the BBFC's activities on this front were causing questions to be raised in Parliament, and on 7 December 1938 the issue was debated in the Commons. The MP who initiated the debate, Geoffrey Mander, complained that 'nothing anti-government, nothing anti-Fascist is permitted, but anything that that is favourable to the policy that the government are pursuing is allowed to go forward'. In 1939 two projects were banned – *Passport for a Girl* and *Swastika* – as was the Soviet anti-Nazi feature *Professor Mamlock*. The BBFC announced its intention to ban this last before it had even been submitted, but the ban was rescinded after the Germans invaded Poland, although a number of cuts were required. By now Hollywood was producing anti-Nazi films, but the BBFC dithered for some time before passing Anatole Litvak's *Confessions of a Nazi Spy*. And even as late as July 1939, it was holding up a project from the Boulting brothers for a film about the persecution of the Protestant pastor Martin Niemoller by the Nazis, proclaiming that 'its exhibition at the present time would be very inexpedient'.[15]

Given the remarkable degree of control which the BBFC exercised over cinematic representations of every aspect of life, but especially of political life, Nicholas Pronay concludes that, up until the outbreak of war:

The cinema screen – the most widely accessible medium of communications to the largest number of the population – was subject to a coherently thought-out and consistently applied politically conscious censorship. If the function of censorship is to act as negative propaganda, preventing firstly, the presentation of arguments which question the premises of policy and their application in practice; preventing secondly, the presentation of alternative interpretations of the causes of the problems to which the government is devising remedies and thirdly, preventing the projecting of alternative solutions, alternative methods and alternative aims to those projected by the government – then the rules operated by the Board manifestly fulfil these criteria too.[16]

Thus, although this may seem quite extraordinary by contemporary standards, Lord Tyrell could say to the Exhibitors' Association in 1937: 'We may take pride in observing that there is not a singe film in London today which deals with any of the burning questions of the day'.[17]

'Engineers of the soul'

After the war, the BBFC became far less concerned with overtly political matters. And, just like the Production Code Administration in America, and for very similar reasons, it had to adapt to changing times and mores. But, additionally, it had to deal with films passed by its US counterpart, which had a more liberal attitude to representations of sex, and more particularly violence, than did the Board, and it was these areas which would now come to dominate its work. But just because the BBFC was no longer concerned with how major political issues such as 'relations between capital and labour' were represented on screen, this most certainly does not mean that they were not concerned with political issues in the broader sense of the term.

Take, for example, its attitude towards two Hollywood productions: the Marlon Brando biker movie *The Wild One* (1953) and *The Blackboard Jungle* (1955). At this time there was a great deal of official concern about juvenile delinquency, and especially about Teddy Boys. Much of the blame for these was laid at the door of popular culture, and of American cinema and pop music in particular. The government ensured that the latter was strictly rationed by the BBC, and it is simply inconceivable that, in such an officially sanctioned climate of reaction and disapproval, the BBFC would have passed these films uncut, even had it been minded to do so. Indeed, in justifying its rejection of *The Wild One*, the BBFC actually cited this very climate:

> Having regard to the present widespread concern about the increase in juvenile crime, the Board is not prepared to pass any film dealing with this subject unless the compensating moral values are so firmly presented as to justify its exhibition to audiences likely to contain (even with an 'X' certificate) a large percentage of young and immature persons. We are of the opinion that *The Wild One*, presenting as it does a spectacle of unbridled hooliganism escaping with no more than mild censure from a police officer, would be likely to exert a harmful influence in that very quarter about which anxiety is felt and would expose the Board to justifiable criticism for certificating a film so potentially dangerous on social grounds.[18]

And when the film was re-presented in 1959, the Board's Secretary John Trevelyan stated:

> We simply dare not risk passing this film at the present time. As you will know, there has been quite a lot of publicity about adolescent gangs in London and elsewhere recently and, while in some ways the present gangs are more vicious than those depicted in the film, the behaviour of Brando and the two gangs to authority and adults generally is of the kind that

provides a dangerous example to those wretched young people
who take every opportunity to throw their weight about.[19]

The film did not receive a certificate until 1967. However, the
previous year the BBFC banned Roger Corman's biker movie
The Wild Angels on very similar grounds.

In Britain *The Blackboard Jungle* was peculiarly disadvantaged
by having as its theme music Bill Haley's 'Rock Around the
Clock', which had already become synonymous here with
teenage depravity and irredeemable Americanisation. The Board
rejected it, even for the newly created X (adults only) certificate
in terms very similar to those in which it had rejected *The
Wild One*:

> The Board is not prepared to pass any film dealing with juvenile
> delinquency or irresponsible juvenile behaviour, whether on
> the streets or in a class-room, unless the moral values stressed by
> the film are sufficiently strong and powerful to counteract the
> harm that may be done by the spectacle of youth out of control
> … We are quite certain that *Blackboard Jungle*, filled as it is with
> scenes of unbridled, revolting hooliganism, would, if shown in
> this country, provoke the strongest criticism from parents and
> all citizens concerned with the welfare of our young people,
> and would also have the most damaging and harmful effects on
> such young people, particularly those between the ages of 16
> and 18 who, even under an 'X' certificate, would be able to see
> the film.[20]

However, this caused a serious row with the film's producer and
distributor, MGM, which had not encountered any difficulties
with the MPAA, and the film was eventually released, albeit cut
by some six minutes. Even in its censored form, however, it was
banned by the local council in Derby.

Clearly films such as these do not raise the same kind of
political issues as say, *Battleship Potemkin* (1925) or *October*

(1928), but nonetheless in a society in which the regulation of personal behaviour by the state is a political issue, and frequently a highly controversial one, the censorship of cinematic representations of personal behaviour is also a political issue, in the broad sense of the term. As Nikolas Rose, following Foucault, has pointed out, in all modern societies, 'the "soul" of the citizen has entered directly into political discourse and the practice of government', and this entails that

> the personal and subjective capacities of citizens have been incorporated into the scope and aspirations of public powers … Governments and parties of all political complexions have formulated policies, set up machinery, established bureaucracies and promoted initiatives to regulate the conduct of citizens by acting upon their mental capacities and propensities.[21]

This is particularly true of modern Britain, and so, whilst once the BBFC consulted specialists in political propaganda and counter-subversion, it now turns to psychologists, psychiatrists, paediatricians and other contemporary 'engineers of the human soul' (as Rose calls them), and is no longer answerable to the Home Office but to the rather softer-sounding Department of Culture, Media and Sport.

Censoring a new technology

The arrival of home video in 1979 posed a considerable problem for the authorities as it unleashed a torrent of material which the BBFC had either cut or banned outright when submitted to them for cinema exhibition, or which most certainly would have been cut or banned had it been submitted. It is often argued that the newer communications technologies are far more difficult to censor than the older ones; however, the way in which the British government dealt with video in the 1980s and would deal with the Internet in the 1990s and the new millennium (one of the subjects of chapter 5) shows that the new communications media are far from censor-proof.

First into action on the video front in the early 1980s was the veteran pro-censorship campaigner Mary Whitehouse, who was greatly helped by a press as censorious as it was sensation-hungry. She was also fortunate that the arrival of video coincided with the arrival of the government of Mrs Thatcher, who clearly saw it as her moral mission to cleanse the country of the legacy of 1960s 'permissiveness'. With MPs' postbags swelling with letters demanding that something must be done, the Director of Public Prosecutions in July 1982 mounted a test case against the videos *S.S. Experiment Camp* (1976), *I Spit on Your Grave* (1978) and *Driller Killer* (1979) in order to test whether the Obscene Publications Act, which had hitherto been used to prosecute only material deemed pornographic, could also be employed successfully against material whose problem, from the authorities' point of view, was violence. They succeeded, and police began raiding video shops the length and breadth of the country in search of what the press, in a decidedly infantile fashion, insisted on calling 'video nasties'. Indeed, in order to assist them, the Director of Public Prosecutions obligingly compiled a list of some sixty titles which his office considered obscene: the first example of an 'Index' in modern Britain. As a consequence, further prosecutions under the Act followed. The problem was, however, that films which were found guilty in certain courts were equally found not guilty in others – *The Evil Dead* (1981) having a particularly chequered history in this respect in the course of its forty-seven appearances in different courts.

As the police raids, parliamentary questions and press hysteria continued, video dealers and distributors began to clear their shelves of offending titles, and the video industry began work on a system of self-regulation. Furthermore, the major Hollywood distributors were now, belatedly, becoming involved in home video, and, in the interests of tapping into the family market and thus maximising their profits, were determined that the fledgling industry clean up its sullied image in Britain as soon as possible.

Nonetheless, those for whom the arrival of home video was clearly a sign of the further moral decline of British society were determined that the industry would not be allowed to regulate itself, and were equally determined to fashion a law which would regulate the new medium far more tightly than the Obscene Publications Act had done thus far. Indeed, bizarre and far-fetched though it may sound, what the Whitehouse brigade and many MPs had in mind was nothing less than a law making it illegal to distribute any video which was not suitable for children. Highly sympathetic though the government of Mrs Thatcher was to the Whitehouse cause, even this hyper-moralistic regime realised that such a measure would have utterly destroyed an increasingly profitable industry, not to mention incurring the wrath not only of Hollywood but also that of the American government, and so eventually the demands of practical reality prevailed.

The resulting Video Recordings Act 1984 required that before any feature film could be distributed on video in Britain, it had to be classified and, if necessary cut, by the BBFC, which also has the power to ban any video outright. The malign shadow of the campaign to ban the distribution of any video not suitable for children can be clearly perceived in the all-important clause of the Act which requires the BBFC to have 'special regard to the likelihood' of videos which it classifies 'being viewed in the home'. In fact, this clause relates not only to the possible presence of children, but also to the fact that the video viewer, unlike the cinema spectator, has the power to replay scenes, or play them in slow-motion, or freeze an individual image, a prospect clearly viewed with alarm and horror by the architects of this legislation. This meant that films on video were even more strictly regulated than films in the cinema.

In the four years after the passing of the Act, the BBFC had to classify every feature film on video that was currently on the market, as well as classify all new releases. The former in itself produced a form of censorship, as many of the smaller distributors either would not or could not pay the considerable classification fees, and so simply withdrew their videos from distribution. This impacted particularly hard on independent and minority-taste films. By 1988, thirty videos rated as U had been cut (1.1% of the total submitted), 130 as PG (5.1%), 188 as 15 (6.7%), 725 as 18 (28.9%) and 56 (30.4%) as R18. Twenty-five were rejected outright. Clearly, then, films in the adult categories were overwhelmingly the main victims of the new system. Bizarrely, it was precisely at this moment that the BBFC changed its name to the British Board of Film Classification, even though it was actually carrying out more censorship than ever before! So although the Video Recordings Act was represented by its creators and a credulous press as simply a means of ridding the country of a few 'video nasties', what it in fact created was a massive and draconian apparatus of state video censorship quite unlike anything existing in any other European country except the Republic of Ireland.[22]

The real beauty of the Act, from the authorities' point of view, is of course its sheer simplicity and the way in which it bypasses the Obscene Publications Act: from 1984 onwards it has been quite simply illegal to supply a feature film on video (and now DVD) without a BBFC certificate. And the penalties for breaking the law are remarkably severe, including an unlimited fine or imprisonment for up to two years; indeed, even supplying a classified DVD or video in breach of its age restriction (for example selling an 18-rated video to a fifteen year old) can result in a fine of £5,000 and up to six months in gaol. Furthermore, the police and trading standards officers have routinely regarded film collectors who swap DVDs and videos as being in the business of 'supply', so terrified teenage horror fans swapping films banned by the BBFC, or even complete versions of films mangled by the BBFC, have frequently found themselves the victims of police raids, their doors kicked in at dawn, their equipment and collections seized, and their names blackened in their local media.[23]

Harm

However, the Act was even further tightened up in 1994 by the stringent amendments made to it by the Criminal Justice and Public Order Act 1994. These were added in the wake of the murder of James Bulger by two other children. Prompted by the exceedingly ill-judged remark by the trial judge that 'I suspect that exposure to violent films may be in part an explanation' for the murder, the press pack once again re-ignited the 'video nasty' panic, at one point pinning the entire blame for this tragic incident on the horror film *Child's Play 3* (1991). Not least because of the pervasive popular mythology which insists otherwise, it does need to be stressed that there is not a scintilla of evidence that the two children who killed James Bulger had ever seen this film, nor even that they watched horror films.[24] Exposure of the truth, however, did absolutely nothing to stop the Video Recordings Act being amended, it now requiring the BBFC, when classifying a video, to

have special regard (among the other relevant factors) to any harm that may be caused to potential viewers or, through their behaviour, to society by the manner in which the work deals with – (a) criminal behaviour; (b) illegal drugs; (c) violent behaviour or incidents; (d) horrific behaviour or incidents; or (e) human sexual activity.

In its Draft Code of Practice the BBFC points out that these criteria represent

> not a break with former policy, but a confirmation of it, since they put on the face of the legislation factors which the Board has been taking into account for many years. The difference now is that the Board can be held accountable, in court if necessary, for failing to apply these criteria with sufficient rigour. This, we said, would concentrate the mind. It has done.[25]

However, whilst it may indeed be the case that the amendment simply put on a statutory footing what the Board had in fact been doing since 1984, the fact remains that Britain, alone in the Western world, and in a distinct throwback to the 'licencers of the press' discussed in chapter 2, practices not only the state censorship of video but lays down in law guidelines as to what content is and is not acceptable. Furthermore, this procedure is premised on the notion that a medium can in some mysterious way 'harm' not only its spectators but society in general, a notion which many would regard as bearing little or no relationship to how they and others *actually* use the media.

Plus ça change ...

Like the MPAA in the States, the BBFC has actually done its best, or has been forced, according to your point of view, to keep abreast of changing standards. For example, on DVD in 2007, of the 2480 films passed at U, only three (0.1% were cut) The figures for the other categories were as shown in Table 1.

However, whilst these figures show that the Board cuts fewer films for domestic consumption than it did in the immediate aftermath of the Video Recordings Act, it also clearly

Table 1 The BBFC and films on DVD in 2007

Category	Total submitted	Number and percentage cut
PG	2,721	8 (0.3%)
12	2,562	2 (0.1%)
15	2,344	14 (0.6%)
18	950	206 (21.7%)
R18	1,159	314 (27.1%)
Rejected	1	

demonstrates that, its name change notwithstanding, it is not a purely classificatory body, and that the majority of cutting still takes place in the two adult categories. And whilst most people would probably agree that children deserve a degree of protection, they would also probably argue that, within reason, adults should be allowed to watch whatever they wish.

As this chapter has attempted to make clear, the BBFC is much more limited by the state in its room for manoeuvre than is its American counterpart. It also needs to be pointed out that the US system is voluntary (subject to the caveats entered in chapter 3) and that American film-makers have been, since 1952, protected by the First Amendment of the Constitution. However, Britain has no written constitution, the system is very far from voluntary, and all attempts to circumvent it have met with determined police action – for example in the case of cinema clubs showing the Andy Warhol/Paul Morrissey film *Flesh* (1969) in 1970 and Pasolini's *Salò* (1975) in 1977. Furthermore, compared with that of other Western democracies, the bulk of the British press is unusually illiberal, and a particular mark of this illiberal stance is the remarkable frequency with which it has called for the censorship of other media; in particular it has consistently attacked the BBFC for being overly liberal and supported campaigners like Mrs Whitehouse and politicians who have wished to see it either take a far tougher line or be entirely replaced by a different agency. This, along with the undimmed powers of the local authorities, several of which (greatly encouraged by the *Daily Mail*) banned David Cronenberg's *Crash* (1996) in 1997, and the existence of the Obscene Publications Act along with police forces more than willing to enforce it, would make it impossible for the BBFC to become a purely classificatory body even if it wished to do so. And then, as the following narrative explains, the BBFC most certainly has to take account of the attitudes of the government of the day.

During the 1990s, BBFC Secretary James Ferman regularly lamented the fact that, with so few local authorities prepared to licence sex shops, the R18 video category was largely unviable. Instead, distributors were opting to have sex videos heavily cut for an 18 certificate when they might well have passed uncut or only slightly trimmed at R18. Thus in 1996 well over ten hours were cut from sex videos in what Ferman called 'the most soul-destroying use of professional expertise yet invented'.[26] Meanwhile, all around the BBFC's offices in the heart of London's Soho, a black market in uncensored videos flourished, with the tacit acceptance of a police force too busy with other matters to wage constant war on porn dealers. The 1997 BBFC Report thus concluded that:

> No society has ever succeeded in stamping out pornography. In the early eighties, a judgement was made by Parliament that the best solution was to regulate it and segregate it, censoring out its harmful elements and removing it from the ambit of those who have no wish to know about it or are to young to understand its sad triviality. Britain has the framework for creating the most sensible regulatory system for pornography in Europe. The current system does credit to nobody.[27]

In 1996, during the dying days of the Conservative government, the police and the Home Office thus agreed to let the BBFC relax its guidelines on the R18. This they hoped would enable the licensed sex shops to compete more effectively with the illegal ones and eventually to drive them out of business. The material now allowed to pass at R18 was still considerably less strong than that to be found anywhere on the continent of Europe, but when, some months after 'New' Labour came to power in May 2007, the new Home Secretary Jack Straw discovered that the BBFC was actually allowing sex films to be sold in sex shops, he was absolutely furious and insisted in no uncertain terms that the BBFC revert forthwith to its previous R18 guidelines. Among other things, this meant that a sex video entitled *Makin' Whoopee!*, which had been granted an interim R18 during the liberalised period, suddenly found itself faced with demands for cuts, on the grounds of obscenity. In July 1998, the distributor took his case to the Video Appeals Committee (a statutory body established by the Video Recordings Act), and won. The Home Office then shifted its position and argued that the problem with the liberalised guidelines was not necessarily that they let through videos which might prove to be obscene but those which could be 'harmful' in the terms of the Video Recordings Act. As a consequence of the appeal, and in spite of continued Home Office opposition, the BBFC drew up new guidelines to a level just below the most explicit shots contained in *Makin' Whoopee!* During this period seven titles examined at these new standards were referred to Ferman, who found them too explicit and insisted on cuts.

At the end of 1998, the embattled Ferman retired, and his place was taken in January 1999 by Robin Duval, who put all R18 work on hold, thus in effect reinstating the original guidelines. In July two distributors took to the Video Appeals Committee several of the titles cut by Ferman the previous year. Once again the grounds for appeal were that the Board had been inconsistent, and once again the distributors won. The BBFC then took the seemingly extraordinary step of requesting a judicial review of its own Appeals Committee. In May 2000 Mr Justice Hooper found for the Committee, the videos were given their certificates, and the BBFC issued guidelines more liberal than those which had so outraged the censorious Straw in the first place. These still stand, although it needs to be made clear that their enforcement still entails the cutting and banning of much material which is entirely permissible in the US and on the continent.[28]

But what needs to be fully understood, however, is that throughout this whole process, the fiction was maintained, both by the Home Office and the BBFC, that the latter was acting entirely independently. This of course would make its serial changes to its guidelines and its taking its own Appeals Committee to court appear completely inexplicable to anyone not realising what was actually going on. The story makes sense only if one understands that the Home Office under Straw repeatedly blocked, and indeed forced into reverse, the changes which the BBFC wished to make to its R18 guidelines, but that the rules of the game – greatly aided by a lazy and indeed complicit press – insisted that the pretence be kept up that the only player involved in the censorship process was the BBFC. Indeed, on 9 December 1997, the *Telegraph* expressed perfectly, although, one suspects, unwittingly, the contradictions inherent in having a state video censor whose legitimacy depends on never being allowed to appear as such, when it noted that: 'There is an arm's length relationship between politicians and the censors, which in many ways is healthy; only in dictatorships do governments decide what people can and cannot watch. But while the politicians are happy for the BBFC to be independent of government, there is a view that under Mr Ferman it has become a law unto itself'. And that, of course, would never do!

5

Blocks and filters

It doesn't seem that long ago that the new communications technologies, and especially the Internet, were being celebrated as the greatest boost to freedom of expression since Johannes Gutenberg invented the printing press in the mid-fifteenth century. As Howard Rheingold put it in 1993 in the first edition of *The Virtual Community*: 'Information can take so many alternative routes when one of the nodes of the network is removed that the Net is almost immortally flexible. It is this flexibility that CMC telecom pioneer John Gilmore referred to when he said, "The Net interprets censorship as damage and routes around it"'[1] Some even believed that the way in which the Internet appeared to challenge the authority of national governments would call into question the validity of the nation-state itself. It was this form of thinking that was exemplified by the Electronic Frontier Foundation's famous Declaration of Independence of Cyberspace which was delivered to the World Economic Forum in Davos in 1996 and which proclaimed:

> Governments of the Industrial World, you weary giants of flesh and steel, I come from Cyberspace, the new home of Mind. On behalf of the future, I ask you of the past to leave us alone. You are not welcome among us. You have no sovereignty where we gather … You have no moral right to rule us nor do you possess any methods of enforcement we have true reason to fear … We must declare our virtual selves immune to your sovereignty, even as we continue to consent to your rule over our bodies. We will spread ourselves across the Planet so that no one can arrest our thoughts.[2]

Keeping a grip

However, even by the time the new edition of Rheingold's book was published in 2000, things had already changed considerably. Note, for instance, how Manuel Castells in his helpful encapsulation of the libertarian vision of the Internet is careful to use the past tense throughout:

> Created as a medium for freedom, in the first years of its worldwide existence the Internet seemed to foreshadow a new age of liberty. Governments could do little to control communication flows able to circumvent geography, and thus political boundaries. Free speech could diffuse throughout the planet, without depending on mass media, as many could interact with many in an unfettered manner. Intellectual property (in music, in publications, in ideas, in technology, in software) had to be shared since it could hardly be enclosed once these creations were placed on the Net. Privacy was protected by the anonymity of communication on the Internet, and by the difficulty of tracing back the sources and identify the content of messages transmitted using Internet protocols.[3]

Of course, it was precisely the global nature of the information flows facilitated by the Internet which caused the greatest consternation around the world amongst those used to keeping a tight grip on the media in their own countries. Authoritarian regimes were hardly likely to welcome an influx of democratic ideas, and much Internet content has clearly proved problematic and unwelcome for many democratic ones too. Both, in fact, have actually found very little difficulty in dealing with indigenous online content of which they disapprove, and they have done so in the same ways that they have traditionally dealt with similar kinds of offline content: passing legislation, identifying and prosecuting producers and distributors, and thus removing the offending content from circulation. The censorship of content produced elsewhere is, of course, more problematic, but, as we shall see, by no means as impossible as cyber-utopians once believed it to be.

On the first Online Free Expression Day, 12 March 2008, Reporters Without Borders noted that that more than 2,600 websites, blogs or discussion forums were closed or made inaccessible in 2007 and that at least sixty-two cyber-dissidents were currently in prison worldwide (forty-eight of them in China). It named its top fifteen 'Internet enemies' as Belarus, Burma, China, Cuba, Egypt, Ethiopia, Iran, North Korea, Saudi Arabia, Syria, Tunisia, Turkmenistan, Uzbekistan, Vietnam and Zimbabwe, and also published a further list of eleven countries 'under watch': Bahrain, Eritrea, Gambia, Jordan, Libya, Malaysia, Sri Lanka, Tajikistan, Thailand, United Arab Emirates and Yemen. Meanwhile the World Information Access Project has calculated that the most dangerous countries in which to be a blogger are China, Egypt and Iran, that from 2003 to 2008 bloggers spent a total of 940 months in jail, and that the average time that a blogger was incarcerated was fifteen months.[4]

The OpenNet Initiative now lists over thirty states which employ various forms of Internet filtering and blocking, a mode of online censorship pioneered by China and Saudi Arabia. Filters were originally developed in the West so that Internet service providers (ISPs), could filter out viruses, worms and spam. They can, however, quite easily be used to filter out other forms of content. The basic procedures are actually relatively simple. For example, filtering can take place at the level of the local Internet cafe. In many countries, people cannot afford to own a computer, and use such cafes instead. Here it is not difficult for governments to insist that cafes install filters on their computers. Thus in Turkey cafe owners must agree in writing to block access to certain sites. Taiwan has regulations that require cafes to block access to pornography and gambling websites. And in certain countries, such as Tunisia and Vietnam, police officers sometimes patrol internet cafes to check what users are viewing.

Better known is the process of national filtering, by which a government denies its citizens access to specific categories of Internet material. Thus in Iran from 2006 onwards, all websites have had to register with the authorities and apply the appropriate filters. All Internet traffic is routed through proxy servers that allow the censors to block by specific URLs. In 2007 around twenty bloggers were arrested on account of their online activities. Yemen uses technology developed by Websense to block pornography. In Singapore ISPs are required to block a list of 100 'high impact' sites, which are mainly pornographic ones. Syria blocks opposition and human rights sites, and also all those with an i.il (Israel) domain suffix. Meanwhile Saudi Arabia has been particularly energetic in blocking pornography, sites which promote drug use or facilitate online gambling, information which would help to circumvent the government-imposed filters, and sites which promote dialogue between Christians and Muslims or are considered generally to be in violation of Islamic tradition. According to a report by the OpenNet Initiative, the Saudi government puts proxy servers between the government-owned Internet backbone and servers outside the country. If a Saudi user requests illicit content from a foreign server, the request travels through the intermediate proxy server where it can be filtered and blocked. This filtering technology was developed by the Secure Computing Corporation, the makers of SmartFilter. Interestingly, when a user receives a message that a page has been blocked, they are invited to suggest other sites that might be blocked. According to the Saudi Internet Services Unit (ISU), there are around 200 such suggestions per day, and about thirty per cent of these are taken up

Content filtering used to be a fairly crude affair. However, with the massive growth of computing power, it is now possible to employ a form of content analysis by means of which content is filtered when keywords or phrases are found within the request for content or within the content itself. This avoids having to filter out entire sites, and is like censoring out individual sentences within books, as opposed to censoring entire books themselves.[5]

China: the Great Firewall and the Golden Shield

Undoubtedly the best-known example of a country which censors the Internet is China, which provides us with a useful case study of all the various ways in which such censorship can be undertaken.

Commercial Internet accounts were first authorised in China in 1995 and by June 2007 China had 147 million Internet users, with a countrywide penetration rate of 10.5% (although there are huge regional variations). By the end of 2006 there were over twenty million bloggers, and in 2007 China had the largest number of Voice-over-Internet Protocol (VoIP) users in the world. So, on one level, the Internet in China is in an extraordinarily healthy state. But what the Chinese government is clearly trying to do is to build an Internet that is free enough to support and maintain its fast-growing economy, and yet controlled enough to lessen threats to its monopoly on power. It has been estimated that some 30,000 police officers are employed to spend their time on the Internet looking for websites (both Chinese and foreign) which should be blocked, as well as trawling through e-mails and chat-rooms searching for illegal keywords. At least twelve different government departments exercise authority over the Internet, including the State Council Information Office, the Ministry of Public Security and the Ministry of Information Industry, the last of which is in charge of the licensing and registration of all Internet content providers. In 2001, Human Rights Watch estimated that the Chinese government had issued more than sixty sets of Internet regulations, but since then many new ones have been issued. However, this powerful framework of national control is only part of the picture, since national regulations coexist with an unknown number of provincial and local regulations, guidelines, policy documents and other legal instruments.

More specifically, as Human Rights Watch explains:

> Internet censorship in the People's Republic of China is overseen technically by the Ministry of Information Industry. Policy about what substantive content is to be censored is largely directed by the State Council Information Office and the Chinese Communist Party's Propaganda Department, with input from other government and public security organs. Physical access to the Internet is provided by nine state-licensed Internet Access Providers (IAPs), each of which has at least one connection to a foreign Internet backbone, and it is through these connections that Chinese Internet users access Internet websites hosted outside of China. The individual Chinese Internet user buys Internet access from one of several thousand Internet Service Providers (ISPs), who are in effect retail sellers of Internet access that is in turn purchased wholesale from the nine IAPs.[6]

Amongst the numerous regulations governing the Internet in China, one of the more detailed in terms of its listing of proscribed content is the Provisions on the Administration of Internet News Information Services issued jointly by the State Council Information Office and the Ministry of Information Industry in September 2005. Article 19 of this measure forbids material:

    (1) violating the basic principles as they are confirmed in the Constitution;

(2) jeopardizing the security of the nation, divulging state secrets, subverting of the national regime or jeopardizing the integrity of the nation's unity;

(3) harming the honour or the interests of the nation;

(4) inciting hatred against peoples, racism against peoples, or disrupting the solidarity of peoples;

(5) disrupting national policies on religion, propagating evil cults and feudal superstitions;

(6) spreading rumours, disturbing social order, or disrupting social stability;

(7) spreading obscenity, pornography, gambling, violence, terror, or abetting the commission of a crime;

(8) insulting or defaming third parties, infringing on the legal rights and interests of third parties;

(9) inciting illegal assemblies, associations, marches, demonstrations, or gatherings that disturb social order;

(10) conducting activities in the name of an illegal civil organization; and

(11) any other content prohibited by law or rules.[7]

However, Article 19 extends in practice well beyond information which might genuinely incite hatred or disturb social order, and is employed to prohibit all reporting that reflects a line different from the official government position, or contains information that the government deems too embarrassing, or is too candid in its discussion of serious social problems.

In order to protect itself from Internet material coming from the outside world China has surrounded itself with the world's most sophisticated information barrier, one which lets in what the government wants and blocks what it doesn't. This 'Great Firewall of China' was built primarily by Cisco, which in the 1990s had developed filtering systems for US companies keen for their employees to have access to the Internet but less keen for them to use it during working hours for their private pleasure. Nearly all Internet data enters or leaves China via fibre-optic cables at three points, and the Chinese government has ordered Chinese Internet carriers to install routers here, which act as gatekeepers by filtering out material deemed illegal. The government provides carriers with a list of all the banned sites, identified by their Internet Protocol (IP) addresses (a numerical identification which is assigned to devices participating in a computer network) and URL (uniform resource identifier – a string of characters used to identify or name a resource on the Internet), and these are simply fed into the filters.

Right from the Internet's beginnings in China, it has been made abundantly clear by the authorities that ISPs based there, whether Chinese or foreign-owned, must themselves actively participate in the regulation process if they wish to remain in business. All Internet Content Providers (ICPs), commercial and non-commercial, are required to register for and display a licence in order to operate legally, and both these and all ISPs are held legally responsible for all content appearing on the websites for which they are responsible, however this content was created. This means that it is not only material coming from outside China which is subject to stringent monitoring and censorship, but all home-produced material too.

China currently has more than 200,000 Internet cafes, all of which are supposed to be licensed. In the early years of the new millennium thousands of unlicensed cafes across the country were shut down. However, at least sixty per cent remain unlicensed, although three governmental departments have the power to shut down any cafes which they deem to be inade-quately policing themselves. This entails installing filtering software, banning minors from entering, monitoring the activi-ties of users, recording every user's identity and keeping session logs for up to sixty days. Cafes also use CCTV cameras to watch what sites their customers are visiting, and put up posters warning them not to visit illegal websites; sometimes police officers patrol the cafes as well.

Inevitably, China has also turned its attention to the new social media (see below). In 2006 over half of China's then 137 million Internet users were found to have visited video sharing sites, and in August that year the State Administration for Radio, Film and Television announced that it would be issuing regulations subjecting all online video content to its inspection. The same year, authorities in the south-western province of Chonqing announced that people publishing on the Internet videos deemed defamatory would be punished.

Since March 2001, all ISPs operating in China have been expected to sign the 'voluntary' *Public Pledge on Self-Discipline for the Chinese Internet Industry*. Initiated by the Internet Society of China, this requires signatories to promise to refrain from 'producing, posting, or disseminating pernicious information that may jeopardize state security and disrupt social stability'.[8] The Internet Society of China is the major professional association for the Chinese Internet industry, but whilst it is called a nongovernmental organisation, its governing body is the Ministry of Information Industry, the government ministry in charge of China's national Internet infrastructure.

Analysis of blocked material shows, unsurprisingly, that this involves subjects which the government believes would endanger national security, conflict with official viewpoints, enable people to contact illegal organisations or organise illegal gatherings, and so on, which means that sites dealing with, for example, Tibetan and Taiwanese independence, human rights, the Tiananmen Square demonstrations and Falun Gong are routinely blocked.[9] Inevitably, the deliberate vagueness of the official proscriptions serves only to encourage ISPs to err on the side of caution, as one of the penalties for transgression is loss of the licence to operate. As Human Rights Watch explains:

The government leaves the exact specifics and methods of censorship up to companies themselves. Companies generate their 'block-lists' based on educated guesswork plus trial-and-error: what they know to be politically sensitive, what they are told in meetings with Chinese officials, and complaints they may receive from Chinese authorities in response to the appearance of politically objectionable search results. But the complicity of companies is even more direct: they actually run diagnostic tests to see which words, phrases, and web addresses are blocked by the Chinese authorities at the router level, and then add them to their lists, without waiting to be asked by the authorities to add them. And because they seek to stay out of trouble and avoid complaints from the authorities, many businesspeople who run ICPs in China confess that they are inclined to err on the side of caution and over-block content which does not clearly violate any specific law or regulation, but which their instincts tell them will displease the authorities who control their license. In all these ways, companies are doing the government's work for it and stifling access to information. Instead of being censored, they have taken on the role of censor.[10]

The extent to which this is indeed the case can be gleaned from the fact that on 9 April 2006

fourteen major Web portals including www.sina.com, www.sohu.com, www.baidu.com, www.tom.com and Yahoo's Chinese website issued a joint declaration calling for the Internet industry to censor 'unhealthy' and 'indecent' information that is 'severely harmful to society', voluntarily accept supervision, and strengthen 'ethical' self regulation. Their proposal sparked a flurry of similar pledges across China, from legal Web sites to blog hosting services, and with targeted content extended to include Party secrets and information affecting national security.[11]

Since it was introduced, the 'pledge' has been signed by over 300 organisations, although Yahoo is the only Western one known to have done so. Reporters Without Borders accused the company of being complicit in 'demolishing the very foundations of the Internet and democracy'[12] and labelled it a 'Chinese police auxiliary'.[13] As Goldsmith and Wu conclude:

> By 2005 Yahoo had come full circle. The darling of the Internet free speech movement had become an agent of thought control for the Chinese government. Yahoo today provides Chinese citizens with a full suite of censored products. Its Chinese search engines do not return full results, but block sites deemed threatening to the public order. Yahoo's popular chat rooms feature software filters designed to catch banned phrases like 'multi-party elections' or 'Taiwanese independence'. It also employs human and software censors to monitor chat room conversations.[14]

Indeed, Human Rights Watch claims that at least four of the fifty-two government critics in gaol in China in 2006 were convicted partly because of disclosure of their personal e-mail accounts by Yahoo.

However, although Yahoo is the only non-Chinese Internet company providing e-mail services with user data hosted inside China, it is by no means the only Western company acting as a censor there. In 2005 Microsoft admitted that its Windows Live Spaces (also known as MSN Spaces), which allows users to set up blogs in China, would automatically block words like 'freedom' and 'democracy'. And when Google, which in China faces stiff competition from the Mandarin search engine Baidu, found that its unfiltered search engine was frequently delayed and disrupted in China – and was entirely blocked for two weeks in September 2002 – it launched Google.cn in January 2006, a filtered search engine especially for China (although it did leave online its Google.com Chinese-language search engine). But as China keeps its instructions and orders for filtering deliberately broad, so, 'in a quintessential act of self-censorship, while Google is given official guidance on what topics to remove from its search service, it has been charged to draw the line for itself in identifying and purging sensitive content', thus becoming 'committed to, if not entrenched in, what now appears to be a *de facto* policy of public-private negotiated transnational filtering at government behest'.[15] Similarly Skype has a Chinese-language version developed and marketed in China by the Chinese company TOM Online, and Skype executives have publicly acknowledged that the TOM-Skype software censors 'sensitive' words in text chats, a practice which they have justified as being in keeping with local 'best practices'.

Thus border control courtesy of Cisco is supplemented by internal controls courtesy of Yahoo, Microsoft and Google, all of whom were censured in February 2006 by a US congressional hearing which accused them of sacrificing principles to profit. Senator Jim Leach of Iowa called Google 'a functionary of the Chinese government', their stock market value plunged, and protests were mounted outside its Californian headquarters. And Human Rights Watch has argued that they and Skype are

> complicit in the Chinese government's censorship of political and religious information and/or the monitoring of peaceful speech in various ways – and, it is important to note, to widely varying degrees. They have all accepted at least some Chinese government demands without mounting any meaningful challenge to them. These are by no means the only multinational companies that currently facilitate Chinese government censorship and surveillance. But they are the most prominent examples, whose contribution to China's censorship regime to date is most well documented and publicly visible.[16]

It is important to grasp that the Great Firewall is in fact but part of a much larger surveillance and control system known as the

Golden Shield. This was first unveiled at the Security China 2000 trade fair held in Beijing in November 2000, and is intended to be a nationwide, digital, database-driven, remote surveillance system offering officials instantaneous access to records on every citizen in China. The United Kingdom, the world leader in CCTV (a crucial part of the Shield), had its own special section in the show, and other eager customers at the fair included Siemens, Motorola (which now supplies China's traffic police with wireless communication devices), Cisco Systems, Sun Microsystems (which has helped to develop a computer network linking China's thirty-three provincial-level police bureaus), and the Canadian company Nortel Networks. This last has played a particularly important role in the construction of the phenomenally costly Shield, mainly by selling to China a version of its 'Personal Internet' initiative, which is designed to enable ISPs to track the online activities of individual Internet users, and which has been heavily criticised by privacy campaigners in the US. Again, the clear and present danger is that systems such as these, which have been developed for commercial purposes in the West in order to deliver increasingly personalised Internet content, can also be used to snoop on Internet users for political purposes (and by no means simply in China, either). Thus while China is undoubtedly conducting its own advanced research and developing home-grown security systems, the IT security field in China remains very heavily dependent on the expertise provided by transnational corporations through joint venture partnerships, technology transfers and direct investment.

The uncomfortable fact that Chinese censorship of the Internet is carried out with the complicity of Western organisations is all too clearly illustrated by the controversy attending the 2008 Olympic Games. In its official bid to host the Games, the Chinese government promised that there would be no restrictions on journalists reporting the event. But when journalists arrived at the Main Press Centre in Beijing at the end of July

2008 they discovered not only that they could not access websites such as Amnesty International, the BBC and Radio Free Asia but also that the International Olympic Committee (IOC), in spite of earlier assurances to journalists that there would be no Internet censorship, had entered into a covert agreement which allowed the Chinese government to block websites which it regarded as not being Games-related. Similarly, the Beijing organisers of the Games suddenly announced that all that had originally been offered was 'sufficient, convenient Internet access for foreign journalists to report the Olympics'. After vociferous complaints from journalists and human rights organisations, a number of sites were unblocked, but the OpenNet Initiative estimated that that on the eve of the games about fifty sites remained blocked, including those of the Committee to Protect Journalists, Human Rights Watch, Human Rights in China, China Digital Times, and the Dui Hua Foundation, which campaigns on behalf of political detainees. Since the end of the Games, a number of unblocked sites have been quietly re-blocked.

Social media and the 'bordered Internet'

Technological advances and the falling cost of digital recording equipment of one kind or another have greatly facilitated the process of sharing user-generated images online – witness the huge growth of sites such as Facebook, Flickr (owned by Yahoo) and YouTube (owned by Google). Social media such as these are more difficult to filter than older forms of Internet communication, partly because of the huge amount of content produced and partly because the multimedia formats involved require much more elaborate forms of filtering in order to identify and block illegal content. Terrorists, delinquents and amateur pornographers have all been quick to make use of these new technologies, and the ease with which it is now possible to distribute a potentially infinite range of material online inevitably produces pressures on providers to police their sites in some way, and not simply as a result of being leaned on by censorship-minded governments. Thus terms of use agreements prohibit users from posting material that many might find offensive, and hosts both monitor content themselves and encourage users to report content which they think should not be there.

However, social media are now heavily used by political activists, and this has obviously attracted the attention of various governments. For example, during the anti-government demonstrations led by Buddhist monks in Burma in 2007, known as the 'Saffron Revolution', both still and moving images of the demonstrations were circulated on social media sites, and this, along with other forms of online protest activity, led the government to try cut off the country entirely from the outside world, shutting down the entire Internet in Burma for the best part of three weeks in September and October. More than a dozen countries (including Brazil, Indonesia, Morocco, Pakistan and Turkey) have at times blocked the entire YouTube site because they disliked the contents of a relatively small number of videos. Such wholesale censorship may be crude, but it can also help to persuade companies concerned about their profits to censor themselves. Thus, for example, in April 2007 the Thai government blocked YouTube because it deemed a number of videos offensive to the King, and thus illegal in Thailand. YouTube's terms of use agreement states that users may not submit material which is contrary to local, national and international laws and regulations, and although it did appear at first to resist the Thai government's demand that it censor itself in order to get the block lifted, by May Google had removed a number of the offending videos, and by August it had created a programme of geo-locational filtering which could be used to block users in

Thailand from viewing such material. This particular example of the 'block or be blocked' dilemma clearly illustrates how companies like YouTube now find themselves engaged in a series of public-private transnational efforts to achieve what is coming to be known as a 'bordered Internet'.

'Computer pornography is a new horror'

Thus far this chapter has focussed on non-Western, and largely non-democratic, countries. However, it would be extremely misleading to give the impression that the Internet in the West is immune to censorship. Here, however, governments have attempted to justify their censorial impulses mainly by recourse to claims that they are attempting to protect children from accessing pornography, although sites containing hate speech, and especially since 9/11, sites allegedly encouraging or abetting terrorism, are frequently cited as well. However, the degree to which these attempts have been successful varies greatly from country to country, as a comparison of the US and the UK will clearly demonstrate.

In both countries, the increasingly widespread availability of the Internet in the 1990s was met with floods of stories about how it was dominated by pornography and, increasingly, child pornography. In the UK, in February 1994, the Home Affairs Select Committee published a report on the subject which opened with the words 'computer pornography is a new horror'[17] and concluded with the recommendation that the government must remain vigilant to the 'threat to the innocence and decency of our children posed by computer pornography'.[18] As the *Guardian* put it on 16 April 1994: 'Forget the video nasty: the latest moral panic is computer porn', and papers were soon awash with greatly exaggerated stories about the extent of this kind of material on the Internet. For example, on 13 September 1995 the *Telegraph* declared in a story headed 'Electronic porn floods network' that 'paedophiles and pornographers are becoming the biggest users of the Internet', adding for good measure that 'half the non-academic material in the "global village" is pornographic', whilst the London *Evening Standard*, 11 October 1995, called the Internet 'a heavily used red-light district, sending pornography into millions of homes'. Indeed by 1996 the dark side of the Internet had become such an over-used journalistic trope that John Naughton, the *Observer*'s specialist in new media, complained in that paper on 9 June that 'to judge from British coverage of the subject, there are basically three Internet stories': 'Cyberporn invades Britain', 'Police crack Internet sex pervert ring', and 'Net addicts lead sad virtual lives'.

Meanwhile in the US in 1995, a report entitled *Marketing Pornography on the Information Superhighway* was published by Carnegie-Mellon graduate student Marty Rimm, which alleged that pornography was 'one of the biggest, if not the biggest, recreational applications of users of computer networks' and that fifteen of the top forty (as measured by traffic volume) Usenet groups distributed pornography. Though the research had not been peer reviewed and lacked a clear methodology, the report received widespread uncritical coverage. Senator Charles E. Grassley drew on it for his much-reported allegation that '83.5 per cent of all computerised photographs available on the Internet are pornographic'[19] and *Time*, 25 June 1995, sensationalised it in a cover feature entitled 'On a screen near you: cyberporn'. As Henry Jenkins aptly put it:

> The figure of the endangered child surfaced powerfully in campaigns for the Communications Decency Act, appearing as a hypnotised young face awash in the eerie glow of the computer terminal on the cover of *Time*, rendering arguments

about the First Amendment beside the point. As one letter to *Time* explained, 'if we lose our kids to cyberporn, free speech won't matter'.[20]

The First Amendment at bay

Largely as a result of articles such as these, and of vigorous lobbying by pro-censorship groups such as Enough is Enough, the Communications Decency Act (CDA) was passed in the US in 1996, making it illegal to distribute via the Internet 'indecent' images or other forms of communication 'in a manner available to a person under 18 years of age'. As in most cases it is impossible accurately to check users' ages, this would have effectively banned all 'indecent' images from all parts of the Internet except those accessed only by credit card. On 26 June 1997 the Supreme Court declared the CDA to be an unconstitutional violation of the First Amendment and argued that 'this new marketplace of ideas', this 'most participatory form of mass speech yet developed', should enjoy exactly the same protection as other forms of communication as it essentially includes all of them. It also argued that less restrictive forms of control, such as blocking and filtering, were available, and that the term 'indecent' was so broad as to threaten with prosecution 'large amounts of nonpornographic material with serious educational or other value'[21] . It also strongly endorsed the American tradition of free expression in its judgement that:

> As a matter of constitutional tradition, in the absence of evidence to the contrary, we presume that governmental regulation of the content of speech is more likely to interfere with the free exchange of ideas than to encourage it. The interest in encouraging freedom of expression in a democratic society outweighs any theoretical but unproven benefit of censorship.[22]

Nothing daunted, however, Congress passed in 1998 the Child Online Protection Act (COPA) which criminalised material deemed 'harmful to minors' by 'contemporary community standards'. Again opponents argued that this had the unconstitutional effect of making it illegal to publish online anything thought unfit for anyone under seventeen, and in 1999 the Court of Appeals for the Third Circuit struck it down as unconstitutional, ruling that applying such standards in cyberspace would inevitably force Internet publishers to comply with the most conservative communities' notions of what was harmful. This was found insufficient by the Supreme Court in 2002, following which in 2003 the Court of Appeals ruled it unconstitutional on the grounds that it improperly restricted access to a substantial amount of online speech that is lawful for adults, also arguing that blocking and filtering were less restrictive ways of shielding children from unsuitable content online. The case returned to the Supreme Court in 2004, which agreed, specifically pointing out that 'filtering's superiority to COPA is confirmed by the explicit findings of the Commission on Child Online Protection, which Congress created to evaluate the relative merits of different means of restricting minors' ability to gain access to harmful materials on the Internet'.[23] The case was then referred back for trial, and on 22 March 2007 District Court Judge Lowell Reed, Jr., invalidated COPA on the grounds that it violated the First Amendment, that the government had not proved that the Act was the least restrictive and most effective way of meeting its objective, and that it was 'impermissibly vague and overbroad'. He also argued that 'perhaps we do the minors of this country harm if the First Amendment protections, which they will with age inherit fully, are chipped away in the name of their protection'.[24]

On one level, then, the existence of blocking and filtering mechanisms actually helped those opposed to COPA. However, in 2000 such mechanisms had received a form of Congressional blessing in the Children's Internet Protection Act, which requires schools and libraries to implement 'Internet safety measures' (namely the filtering and blocking of material deemed 'harmful to minors') if they wish to receive federal aid for their computing provision. By this point, in fact, many schools and libraries were already engaging in such practices, usually at the behest of their local authorities. The problem with such systems, however, is that their use is generally marked by a lack of transparency and public scrutiny, not least because lists of blocked sites are the intellectual property of the company that created the software. (N2H2, the maker of the Bess system, has a forty per cent market share in this field.) Furthermore, the filtering process is frequently crude and over-inclusive, and parents and young people in the US have frequently complained about the wide range of material filtered out, which has variously included the Declaration of Independence, the *Qu'ran*, Shakespeare's plays, *The Owl and the Pussycat*, *The Adventures of Sherlock Holmes*, *The Grapes of Wrath*, and websites relating to HIV/AIDS, breast cancer, anorexia and child labour.

A democratic deficit

In the UK, where the will to censor is deeply ingrained in the culture, and where the unwritten rubric runs that the more popular a form of communication, the more it needs to be controlled, the Internet was always going to be a problem for the censorious and authoritarian. And so, when the Internet first became a truly popular medium in the UK, the authorities determinedly applied pressure to the Internet at its most vulnerable point: the intermediary. In other words, the individual ISP. As Jack Goldsmith and Tim Wu point out:

> Internet Service Providers are the obvious first target for a strategy of intermediary control. It can be great fun to talk about the

Internet as a formless cyberspace. But ... underneath it all is an ugly physical transport infrastructure: copper wires, fibre-optic cables, and the specialised routers and switches that direct information from place to place. The physical network is by necessity a local asset, owned by phone companies, cable companies, and other service providers who are already some of the most regulated companies on earth. This makes ISPs the most important and most obvious gatekeepers to the Internet. Governments can achieve a large degree of control by focusing on the most important ISPs that service the majority of Internet users.[25]

In Britain ISPs were originally regarded as publishers of the material which they carry, and thus as legally responsible for it, even though most of it is provided by third parties. However, according to the EU E-Commerce Directive which came into force in 2000 (although not until 2002 in the UK), ISPs are in fact 'mere conduits', carriers of information rather like the postal services. It thus recognises that an ISP is not a publisher, and does not have editorial control over material posted on its servers by third parties. On the other hand, if an ISP obtains 'actual knowledge' of illegal content held on their servers and fails to remove it, then they render themselves liable to prosecution. This does indeed take a certain amount of pressure off ISPs, but it also renders them extremely vulnerable to pressure from corporate interests, law enforcement agencies and self-regulatory bodies such as the Internet Watch Foundation (see below), who have only to allege that material is illegal for ISPs to become understandably nervous about carrying it. And if they then decide to take it down they effectively become a regulatory agent, thus to a significant extent *privatising* the process of online censorship.[26]

In Britain, the initial responsibility for investigating pornography on the Internet fell to the Clubs and Vice Unit at Charing

Cross Police Station in London. On 9 August 1996, the Unit's Chief Inspector Stephen French wrote to some 140 ISPs listing 133 newsgroups which the police wanted them to block on the grounds that 'we believe [they] contain pornographic material'. The letter continued:

> This list is not exhaustive and we are looking to you to monitor your Newsgroups identifying and taking necessary action against those others found to contain such material. As you will be aware the publication of obscene articles is an offence. This list is only the starting point and we hope, with the co-operation and assistance of the industry and your trade organisations, to be moving quickly towards the eradication of this type of Newsgroup from the Internet … We are very anxious that all service providers should be taking positive action now, whether or not they are members of a trade association. We trust that with your co-operation and self regulation it will not be necessary for us to move to an enforcement policy.[27]

However, the list was arranged so that the first half page consisted of unambiguously titled paedophile newsgroups, access to which many people doubtless would want banned. It was only by reading on that it appeared that the police wanted to restrict access to other kinds of newsgroups as well, if titles such as alt.binaries.pictures.erotica.cheerleaders and alt.binaries. pictures.erotic.centerfolds are anything to go by, which hardly suggest material which would fall foul of the Obscene Publications Act, and were doing so without prior debate in Parliament or elsewhere. However, the police, who appeared to be doing their best to create and not simply to enforce the law, were not acting entirely off their own bat. As Alan Travis, the *Guardian*'s Home Affairs editor, explains:

> The Conservative Science and Industry Minister at the time, Ian Taylor, underlined the explicit threat to ISPs if they did not

close down the newsgroups in question. He warned that the police would act against any company that provided their users with pornographic or violent material. He went on to make it clear that there would be calls for legislation to regulate all aspects of the Internet unless service providers were seen wholeheartedly to embrace responsible self-regulation.[28]

The direct result of what can only be described as a campaign of threats and bullying was that in September 1996 the major ISPs set up the Internet Watch Foundation (IWF, initially known as the Safety Net Foundation), a self-regulatory industry body to which members of the public could report Internet content which they deemed illegal, particularly in the area of child pornography. However, after three years the government decided that the IWF was insufficiently effective and its workings were reviewed for the Department of Trade and Industry (DTI) and the Home Office by the consultants KPMG and Denton Hall. As a result, a number of changes were made to the organisation's role and structure, and it was re-launched in early 2000, endorsed by the government and the DTI, which played a 'facilitating role in its creation' according to a DTI spokesman. At the time, Patricia Hewitt, then Minister for E-Commerce, gave it her blessing by stating that 'the Internet Watch Foundation plays a vital role in combating criminal material on the Net'.

Today the IWF describes itself on its website as

the UK's Internet 'Hotline' for the public and IT professionals to report potentially illegal online content within our remit. We work in partnership with the online industry, law enforcement, government, the education sector, charities, international partners and the public to minimise the availability of this content, specifically, child sexual abuse content hosted anywhere in the world and criminally obscene and incitement to racial hatred content hosted in the UK.[29]

It defines sexual abuse content by reference to the UK Sentencing Guidelines Council, which established five levels of seriousness for sentencing for offences involving pornographic images of children. In ascending order, these are:

Level 1. Images depicting erotic posing with no sexual activity.
Level 2. Non-penetrative sexual activity between children, or solo masturbation by a child.
Level 3. Non-penetrative sexual activity between adults and children.
Level 4. Penetrative sexual activity involving a child or children, or both children and adults.
Level 5. Sadism or penetration of, or by, an animal.[30]

The IWF also explains that:

We help Internet service providers and hosting companies to combat abuse of their networks through our national 'notice and take-down' service which alerts them to potentially illegal content within our remit on their systems and we provide unique data to law enforcement partners in the UK and abroad to assist investigations into the distributors of potentially illegal online content.[31]

What this means in practice is that once the IWF has reported to the police the presence on the website of a UK-based ISP content which it deems illegal, that ISP will have no excuse in law that it was unaware of the presence of this material. That this is indeed the case was spelled out by the Department of Trade and Industry Document published in 1998, *Net Benefit: the Electronic Commerce Agenda for the UK*:

Primary responsibility for illegal material on the Internet would clearly lie with the individual or entity posting it. Under UK law, however, an Internet service provider (ISP) which has been made aware of the illegal material (or activity) and has

failed to take reasonable steps to remove the material could also
be liable to prosecution as an accessory to a crime.[32]

In the highly unlikely event that an ISP ignores the IWF's
service it will be contacted by the police and told to remove it
or face prosecution.

The IWF also compiles and maintains a blacklist of mainly
child pornography URLs, which is updated twice daily and
circulated to all UK ISPs, who then block access to the offending material. In this area too the IWF depends largely on reports
from the public, although before being blacklisted, sites will be
examined by a team of analysts trained by the police. At any one
time the list contains between 800 and 1,200 child pornography
URLs, with between 65 and 80 new ones added each week. In
2004 BT introduced its Cleanfeed blocking technology, and by
2006, 90% of British ISPs were using this to block websites on
the IWF blacklist, or were preparing to do so. Cleanfeed is
essentially a server hosting a filter that checks URLs for websites
on the IWF list and returns the message 'website not found' in
the case of positive matches. However, on 15 May 2006, Home
Office minister Vernon Coaker stated in a written answer:

> We recognise the progress that has been made as a result of the
> industry's commitment and investment so far. However, 90 per
> cent of connections is not enough and we are setting a target
> that by the end of 2007, all ISPs offering broadband Internet
> connectivity to the UK general public put in place technical
> measures that prevent their customers accessing websites
> containing illegal images of child abuse identified by the IWF.
> For new ISPs or services, we would expect them to put in place
> measures within nine months of offering the service to the
> public. If it appears that we are not going to meet our target
> through co-operation, we will review the options for stopping
> UK residents accessing websites on the IWF list.

At the time of writing, the figure stands at 95%.

The IWF dislikes being called a censor, and, strictly speaking, it isn't one. But, on the other hand, there cannot be the slightest doubt that it is involved in a process whose end result is self-censorship by ISPs understandably terrified of being accused of distributing child pornography – and, it might be added, keen to burnish their public image as responsible, family-friendly companies and, thus garlanded, to proceed unhindered with the all-important business of making money. But what its existence does is to disguise and obscure the fact that the state is involved in the censorship of the Internet, albeit covertly and at one remove, and its workings make it largely impossible for the authors of online material deemed illegal to defend themselves in court. Furthermore, although it was originally set up and now operates with strong governmental support, its workings have never been the subject of any sustained parliamentary or public scrutiny or debate. But, there again, why should they be? The IWF does not enjoy even the dubious status of a quango, and indeed takes considerable pains to stress that it is a purely private body. The problem, however, is that as such it lacks any kind of democratic legitimacy and authority for its actions. Furthermore, as the addition of 'criminally obscene and incitement to racial hatred content' to the IWF's remit ably testifies, ill-defined bodies such as this are all too prone to the process of mission creep whereby, without any proper public discussion, they quietly expand the range of their activities – usually under pressure from government.

Of course, one of the main problems in the UK is that the obsessive stress on combating child pornography on the Internet has actively discouraged critical discussion of both Internet regulation in general and of the role of the IWF in particular, as few, quite understandably, are keen to run the risk of being painted as 'soft' on this matter. In this respect, it is indeed difficult to disagree with Laurence O'Toole's contention that 'the suspicion remains that the issue of child porn was exploited as part of a bid to gain leverage over this new, unregulated technology, in order to get things under control'.[33] It is also important to bear in mind the very basic (but usually overlooked) point raised by Yaman Akdeniz when he notes that 'child pornography is not an Internet-specific problem and it remains rather as a problem within society. It should be dealt with accordingly, and not specifically in relation to the Internet. The Internet is just another convenient tool for paedophiles who wish to traffic in these kind of materials'.[34]

It is, of course, perfectly right and proper to use the Internet as a means of tracking down those who actually engage in child abuse (or any other kind of non-consensual sexual activity, for that matter). But whether the online existence of such material, and indeed of other material of which the authorities disapprove (seemingly an ever-growing list), serves as virtually an automatic justification for cracking down on freedom of expression on the Internet, is a topic which deserves far more serious and measured public consideration than it has received thus far. And the need for public debate on this matter becomes more pressing the more obvious it becomes that the government intends cracking down on online material other than blatant child abuse images (which very few would wish to defend). However, as the Internet Service Providers Association quite rightly suggests, if this is what the government wants – and in particular if it is going to insist on the imposition of any filtering or censorship processes above the consumer level – it should be open about wishing to impose state censorship on the Internet and not covertly pressurise the ISPs into doing their dirty work for them:

> ISPs are not qualified, sufficiently authorised or resourced to decide on the legality of all the material on the Internet. Whilst ISPs take swift action when they are aware of child pornography on their servers – because it is illegal 'full stop'

both in the UK and throughout the world – not all sorts of material are as easily identifiable as illegal such as instances of libel or defamation.[35]

Indeed, in this respect a major problem with the guidelines with which the IWF operates is that many would question whether images which are taken as falling into Level 1 above necessarily constitute child pornography at all. This is particularly the case since the Sexual Offences Act 2003 changed the legal definition of a child from a person under sixteen (as defined by the Protection of Children Act 1978) to eighteen. This means that it is now a crime to take, make, permit to take, distribute, show, possess with intent to distribute, or to advertise indecent photographs or pseudo-photographs of any person below or apparently below the age of 18. The situation is made even more grave by the fact that under such legislation the offences cover images of young people under eighteen which are deemed merely indecent, a concept which the courts have proved worryingly unable to define except in the broadest terms such as 'offending against recognised standards of propriety' or 'shocking, disgusting and revolting ordinary people'. Seventeen-year-old models on Facebook and YouTube should take note. All of this might matter less if the police could be relied upon to enforce the legislation sensibly and proportionately – however, the numerous occasions on which they have questioned people for photographing their children at bath-time and harassed galleries showing photos of children taken by artists such as Robert Mapplethorpe, Sally Mann, Tierney Gieron and Nan Goldin, show that they absolutely cannot be trusted to do any such thing. Fortunately, in most of these cases the wiser counsels of the DPP have prevailed (much to the fury of the police), but, of course, the beauty of the IWF take-down notices and blacklist, from the police point of view, is that it simply keeps the DPP and the courts (along with any form of proper public scrutiny) out of the loop altogether.

All of these many problems relating to both the authority of the IWF and the nature of its judgements were thrown into the sharpest relief on 5 December 2008 when the IWF decided to take on that bastion of free expression and democratic speech on the Internet, Wikipedia.

Following a single complaint, the IWF blacklisted a Wikipedia article containing an image of the cover of the Scorpions album *Virgin Killer*, which depicts a naked pre-pubescent girl; this it regarded as coming within the Level 1 (erotic posing) category of images outlined above. The decision was taken in consultation with law enforcement in the shape of the Child Exploitation and Online Protection agency (CEOP). In a dramatic demonstration of the censorship capabilities of the Cleanfeed system, the page almost immediately became unavailable to the vast bulk of British users of the Internet. Furthermore, for related technical reasons they found themselves unable to edit other parts of the site, and in some cases access to the whole site slowed to a crawl. Following this, the IWF also received a complaint about the same image being available on the Amazon website. However, rather than blocking the commercial online giant in one of its busiest weeks of the year, following representations from Wikipedia it reversed its original decision on 10 December 'in the light of the length of time the image has existed and its wide availability'.

This isn't exactly convincing, to put it mildly: either the IWF and CEOP think an image is illegal, or they think it isn't. A rather more likely explanation for the IWF's volte-face is that, utterly unused to having its decisions challenged, it simply backed down before the situation spiralled out of its control. In many ways it is a pity that the IWF lacked the courage of its convictions, as a legal challenge to its actions would have helped to clarify the important issues of legitimacy, accountability, expertise and transparency raised in the latter part of this chapter.

6

Markets and moguls

Ever since the advent of neo-liberalism in the 1980s in the US and the UK, the idea has taken hold in many influential media circles that the market is the enemy of censorship (which is seen solely as the prerogative of the state) and the only true friend of freedom of expression. As Rupert Murdoch put it in a highly controversial lecture at the Edinburgh Television Festival in 1989:

> Government control will become increasingly impossible in the new age of television. The multiplicity of channels means that the government thought-police, in whatever form, whether it is the benign good and the great in Britain, or the jackboot-in-the-night elsewhere, will find it hard to control more and more channels. Across the world there is a realisation that only market economies can deliver both political freedom and economic well-being.[1]

On the other hand, an increasing number of media practitioners, scholars and critics have begun to advance the view that unregulated market forces are equally effective as censors of the media as are governments, albeit in a different fashion.

'Diverse and antagonistic sources'

In Western Europe, up until the 1980s, it was generally accepted as axiomatic that broadcasting was simply too important to social well-being and cultural identity to be left entirely to the market. It was also argued that as the airwaves were a scarce resource, a form of 'natural monopoly', they should be used for the public good and not simply as a source of private profit. Broadcasting, whether commercially or publicly funded, was thus regulated by various forms of state or state-appointed bodies according to public service principles. Some of these were intended to keep out certain forms of content deemed undesirable or harmful – and these could indeed be seen as agents of censorship – but others were designed to regulate *into* the system qualities generally regarded as positive, such as, in programming terms, impartiality, independence, originality, innovation and diversity, and in terms of ownership, plurality and public accountability, as it was assumed that plurality of ownership was necessary in order to safeguard diversity – and independence – of content. Such thinking dominated the regulation of broadcasting in Britain until the Broadcasting Act 1990 began the 'deregulation' of the system.[2] The one-time dominant European view has been summed up concisely by Gillian Doyle who points out that:

Recognition of society's need for 'pluralism' and of the threat to pluralism posed by media concentrations has, historically, provided the main impetus for regulating ownership of the media … One of the main concerns surrounding concentrations of media ownership is the risk for democracy and for the wider political system when individual 'voices' gain excessive control over the media. Democracy is threatened if individual media owners, with the power to propagate a single political viewpoint, are allowed to predominate over the supply of media. Cultural pluralism is another important concern. Cultural diversity and the cohesiveness of society will be threatened unless the cultures, views and values of all groupings within society (such as those sharing a particular language, race or creed) are reflected within the media.[3]

Meanwhile, in the US, broadcasting has always been for the most part an entirely commercial matter, but it was nonetheless regulated by the Federal Communications Commission (FCC), which traditionally interpreted the First Amendment as requiring both the prevention of the formation of media monopolies and the maintenance of a diversity of viewpoints which citizens could readily access. The American courts took a similar attitude in the fields of both broadcasting and the written press. The best example of the application of the First Amendment to the press in this respect is that provided by Justice Hugo Black's celebrated judgement in the classic case of *Associated Press v. United States* in 1945, in which Associated Press was found guilty of breaching anti-trust laws by preventing rival newspapers from accessing its copyrighted news services. As Black argued, the First Amendment

> rests on the assumption that the widest possible dissemination of information from diverse and antagonistic sources is essential to the welfare of the public, that a free press is a condition of a free society. Surely a command that the government itself shall not impede the free flow of ideas does not afford nongovernmental combinations a refuge if they impose restraints upon that constitutionally guaranteed freedom … Freedom to publish means freedom for all, and not for some. Freedom to publish is guaranteed by the Constitution, but freedom to combine to keep others from publishing is not. Freedom of the press from governmental interference under the First Amendment does not sanction repression of that freedom by private interests.[4]

Similarly, in another celebrated case, *Red Lion Broadcasting Co. v. FCC* , in which in 1966 the broadcaster argued that the FCC's 'fairness doctrine' infringed the station's constitutional right to free speech, the Supreme Court ruled that because broadcasting frequencies were scarce, the government was 'permitted to put restraints on licensees in favour of others whose views should be expressed on this unique medium'. In the Court's view, then, the licensee had no constitutional right to 'monopolise a radio frequency to the exclusion of his fellow citizens', and the collective right of the viewers and listeners 'to have the medium function consistently with the ends and purposes of the First Amendment' took precedence over the right of the broadcasters to act entirely as they wished. The Court concluded that: 'It is the purpose of the First Amendment to preserve an uninhibited market-place of ideas in which truth will ultimately prevail, rather than to countenance monopolisation of that market, whether it be by the Government itself or a private licensee'.[5]

This market place was seen to depend precisely on the existence of Justice Black's 'diverse and antagonistic sources'. Thus in 1965 the FCC stressed the importance of 'maximum diffusion of control of the media of mass communications'[6] and in 1970 it stated that:

> A proper objective is the maximum diversity of ownership ...
> We are of the view that 60 different licensees are more desirable than 50, and even that 51 are more desirable than 50 ... It might be the 51st licensee that would become the communication channel for a solution to a severe social crisis.[7]

Likewise in 1978 the Supreme Court held that strict limits on media ownership were necessary to prevent an undue concentration of economic power. Indeed, up until the Telecommunications Act 1996 it appeared to be taken as axiomatic that rules to prevent media concentration were fundamental to the health of American democracy and indeed were expressions of fundamental constitutional values. As C. Edwin Baker puts it in the most authoritative study of media ownership published to date:

> In any local, state, or national community, concentrated media ownership creates the possibility of an individual decision

maker exercising enormous, unequal and hence undemocratic, largely unchecked, potentially irresponsible power. History exhibits countless instances of abuse of concentrated communicative power in this and other countries at either local or national levels. Historical stories, however, are not crucial here. Even if this power were seldom if ever exercised, the democratic safeguard value amounts to an assertion that *no democracy should risk the danger*. The Constitution delineates three separate branches, the system of 'separation of powers'. The separation is, in part, a structural means to reduce the risk of abuses of power in government. So too should a country structure the fourth estate. The widest possible dispersal of media power reduces the risk of the abuse of communicative power in choosing or controlling the government.[8]

In other words, it is a key principle that democracy requires media diversity as a structural and systemic safeguard.

Re-regulation

Nonetheless, in recent years, both the FCC and the courts have increasingly taken the line that restrictions on media ownership actually constitute a breach of the First Amendment. Most notably, in 2003 in a review of its broadcast ownership rules, the FCC stated that in future it would seek to minimise their impact on the 'right of speakers to disseminate a message' and did not regard these rules as a 'reasonable means to accomplish ... public interest purposes'. In doing so, it argued, it would be showing 'greater deference to First Amendment interests'.[9] This was followed almost immediately by increased levels of concentration of ownership – and also by a very considerable public and political backlash, which is still reverberating at the time of writing.

As one of the leading American media scholars, Robert McChesney, has argued:

> In the hands of the wealthy, the advertisers, and the corporate media, the newfangled First Amendment takes on an almost Orwellian cast. On the one hand, it defends the right of the wealthy few to effectively control our electoral system, thereby taking the risk out of democracy for the rich and making a farce out of it for most everyone else. And these semi-monopolistic corporations that brandish the Constitution as their personal property eschew any public service obligations and claim that public efforts to demand them violate their First Amendment rights, which in their view means their unimpeded ability to maximise profits regardless of their social consequences. Indeed, the media giants use their First Amendment protection not to battle for open information but to battle to protect their corporate privileges and subsidies.[10]

However, as noted above, this process of 'deregulation' and commercialisation of the media was by no means confined to America. Furthermore, it needs also to be understood as a process of *re-regulation*, whereby regulations originally designed to protect and enhance citizens' communicative rights are being replaced by measures designed to further the interests of media corporations. So how and why did this process come about?

In the 1980s, the traditional 'heavy' industries had begun to decline, and the manufacturing sector was increasingly giving way to the service sector. Governments began to perceive the communications industries as increasingly central to the success of contemporary capitalism – both as transmitters of information of all kinds (and especially money) but also as sources of jobs and hence tax revenue. Their employees were also perceived by right-wing governments, such as Thatcher's, as a good deal less 'militant' and more compliant than miners and steelworkers. At the same time, as their traditional markets became increasingly saturated, the major industrial players cast around to develop new products and services, and to enter new markets both at home and abroad. The electronic media sector looked particularly inviting, not least as new technological developments such as cable and satellite appeared to spell the end of broadcasting as a 'natural monopoly' – something which had always underpinned arguments for public service broadcasting in Europe. Meanwhile, the future possibilities for financial gain offered by 'convergence', in other words the coming together of telecommunications, broadcasting and computing, or, to put it another way, the phone, the television and the home computer, looked like an absolute gold mine. However, to develop the necessary technology and infrastructure would take considerable capital investment, and the last thing which the new media providers wanted was to be saddled with what they perceived as onerous public service requirements. Thus, in return for their capital investment, the new arrivals demanded that the broadcast and telecommunications sectors be 'deregulated' – for which euphemism read re-regulated according to business-friendly principles. Particularly in a Britain led by a government animated by detestation of all things public, they were of course knocking at a wide-open door.

In this vision of things, society is perceived as consisting primarily of a network of providers and recipients of goods and services. Communication services of all kinds increasingly come to be seen as commodities first and foremost, as opposed to public utilities, with private profitability taking precedence over public accessibility. Media audiences are viewed not as citizens with the right to be informed but as consumption units to whom goods and services need to be sold. This attitude was expressed in its crudest and most crass form by the head of the FCC Mark Fowler, in 1984 when he stated that: 'Television is just another appliance. It's a toaster with pictures'.[11] As Sue Curry Jansen puts it:

Under information-capitalism, the marketplace of ideas is no longer a public utility which serves all who seek its goods. Increasingly it becomes a private enterprise which serves only those who can afford to pay a price for the commodities it markets to citizen/shoppers. Under this new system of capitalism, the production of knowledge becomes a basic industry like the production of oil, steel, and transportation.[12]

The media marketplace

What needs to be understood, though, is that making information available to people is an activity of a quite different order than making available, say, cans of peas, in that it is essentially a social good. It thus matters greatly if, as many have claimed, the communications market by no means guarantees that everyone's tastes will be catered for; that certain kinds of material are indeed widely disseminated but that others hardly figure at all; and that differences in the availability of ideas have little to do with their social worth and everything to do with their profitability – in particular their attractiveness to advertisers, who are the real drivers of such a system.

One of the major problems with the argument that a free market media system is the most effective guarantor of freedom of expression is that such a system contains all the same defects as the market system in general (faults to which its more zealous proponents are either blind or indifferent). In particular, 'free market' philosophy is notoriously oblivious to the fact that access to the market is heavily skewed by already-existing inequalities in society among both producers and consumers. Thus the media marketplace is no more open to everyone who wishes to communicate their ideas than is the wider market to anyone who wants to sell goods and services. Indeed, unregulated competition by no means necessarily ensures that new producers are free to enter the marketplace, and media markets in particular are notoriously 'uncontestable' (that is, hard for new entrants to penetrate) because of the extremely high levels of investment needed for entry. Furthermore, existing players in the market, far from welcoming new competitors with open arms (as 'free market' theory would suggest), do their absolute utmost to strangle them at birth through various forms of preda-tion. For example, when in 1987 Robert Maxwell launched Britain's first 24 hour newspaper, the *London Daily News*, Associated Newspapers, who owned London's monopoly paper the *Evening Standard*, immediately launched a 'spoiler' in the form of the *Evening News* which, needless to say, vanished the moment the *London Daily News* collapsed. Similarly when in 2006 Rupert Murdoch's News International launched the freesheet *thelondonpaper* it found itself joined on the street remarkably quickly by Associated's all too aptly titled *London Lite*. On the other hand, Murdoch himself had done his best in 1993 to destroy the *Independent* and *Telegraph* by predatory pricing, using cross-subsidy from elsewhere in his multi-media empire to enable him drastically to cut the price of *The Times*.[13]

Here again one encounters the difficulties involved in simply transferring First Amendment (in the US) and free speech (in Europe) arguments wholesale into discussions of media freedom. This is because individual speech is actually quite different from mediated communication, as McChesney points out:

> It is one thing to assure individuals the right to say whatever they please without fear of government regulation or worse. This is a right that can be enjoyed by everyone on a relatively equal basis. Anyone can find a street corner to stand on to pontificate. It is another thing to say that any individual has the right to establish a free press to disseminate free speech indus-trially to a broader audience than could be reached by the spoken word. Here, to the extent that the effective capacity to

engage in a free press is quite low for a significant portion of the population, the free speech analogy weakens. Moreover, those with the capacity to engage in a free press are in a position to determine who is empowered to disseminate speech to the great mass of the citizens and who is not. This accords special privileges to some citizens who can then dominate public debate.[14]

Or as the journalist and press critic A.J. Liebling succinctly put it in 1947: 'Freedom of the press belongs to those who own one'.[15]

The new media giants

Indeed, one of the major problems with 'deregulating' media markets is that it leads not simply to the concentration of ownership within individual media but across different media as well. Such concentrations are known as oligopolies. 'Deregulation' may indeed enable new players to enter the media, but these tend not to be small, independent companies which might breathe new life into the system, but vast non-media conglomerates. Indeed, in the UK as far back as 1977 the last Royal Commission on the Press, hardly a radical body, was forced to conclude that: 'Rather than saying that the press has other business interests, it would be truer to argue that the press has become a subsidiary of other interests'.[16] There are numerous dangers posed by such a development. For example, those who run such conglomerates may well view their media acquisitions simply as a source of profit as opposed to a source of genuinely informative journalism or quality programming. Equally, they may see them as a source of PR for their other business interests, resulting not simply in the unsavoury spectacle of one branch of a conglomerate providing another with free advertising dressed up as independent editorial, but also putting criticism of those interests effectively out of the reach of the media in its ownership. Put simply, the more a conglomerate owns, the less its media can scrutinise. Worse still, the more the media enmesh themselves in big business – or rather, the more they themselves simply *become* big business – the less able are they to operate as the Fourth Estate is supposed to do, namely to act as a watchdog over state and corporate power. As Steven Barnett and Ivor Gaber argue, in the UK recent years have seen

> a growing interdependence of media entrepreneurs and political parties for their own respective self-advancements. Senior politicians have become more and more convinced (whether rightly or not) of the power of the media and have therefore sought to create harmonious relationships with a few elite owners. Simultaneously, electronic and market developments in the media have raised important legislative issues (for example, on cross-ownership and pay-TV access) which have made it more imperative for owners seeking government favours to ensure productive relationships with ruling parties.[17]

Or as James Curran puts it:

> The press is now organised into large corporations, whose profitability is affected by policy outcomes of a greatly enlarged government. The government, in turn, is affected by the editorial positions of the press, not least because ministers operate in a turbulent environment, no longer stabilised by strong class loyalties, corporatist conciliation and mass party machines. This produces a situation in which press scrutiny of government, and official policy on the press, can be significantly influenced by calculations of mutual advantage. This is a far cry from the simple liberal image of the press as a 'public sentinel', whose critical independence is secured through freedom of the market.[18]

That such a situation greatly encourages the media to censor themselves is all too obvious. (For examples of this process at work see the sections below on Murdoch and Berlusconi).[19]

The restructuring of the media industry (via 'deregulation') has allowed media conglomerates to use their size to pursue strategies not generally available to smaller competitors. They can access vast amounts of investment capital for expensive projects, heavily advertise their products, cross-promote them in their own media, and generally take advantage of the efficiencies resulting from economies of scale, for example absorbing losses on some projects by making up for it with a few blockbuster hits.

One consequence of economies of scale is of course what companies describe as 'downsizing', otherwise known as firing employees, which frequently involves transferring them from the corporate payroll onto the state payroll known as the dole, as happened when Murdoch transferred his newspaper business to Wapping in 1986.[20] In Britain huge numbers of jobs have been lost as ITV, largely as a consequence of the Broadcasting Act 1993 and Communications Act 2003, has gradually abandoned its federal structure, with Carlton and Granada first of all buying up the vast majority of regional franchises and then themselves merging. At the time of writing it has announced plans to scale back drastically the amount of local news which it produces, for reasons which are almost entirely financial. Meanwhile in the local press, the number of publishing companies declined from 200 in 1992 to eighty-five in 2006. In 2003, the twenty largest groups owned eighty-five per cent of regional titles and controlled ninety-six per cent of weekly circulation. The five largest groups – Trinity Mirror, Newsquest, Northcliffe Newspapers, Johnston Press and Archant – own seventy-six per cent of newspaper circulation. Regional monopolies and 'cluster publishing' have developed as big owners have tacitly carved up the country between themselves, and local and regional synergies now mean that some local freesheets now employ literally no journalists at all, with content being simply pasted in from syndicated sources or from the owners' other local papers in the area. (Jack Daw is a common by-line in the press.) The Communications Act 2003 has made it easier for local cross-media concentration to take place. All these developments amount to a degree of regional and local news impoverishment which can certainly be regarded as a form of censorship – not least of a form of media provision which every reliable survey shows that people value very highly indeed.[21]

Market failure

Corporate and political proponents of a 'deregulated' media system usually argue that it will give people more choice than does a regulated one, or, more simply, that it will 'give people what they want'. Thus Murdoch in his MacTaggart lecture boasted that 'we see ourselves as destroyers of monopoly power and as creators of choice' and that he was freeing television and 'placing it in the hands of those who should control it – the people'.[22] However, many people would argue that behind this kind of seemingly democratic but actually thoroughly populist rhetoric lies the simple desire to make a very fast and very big buck. Furthermore, as the Pilkington Report into British broadcasting forthrightly asserted in 1960, rhetoric of this kind (which has a long history) is in fact

> patronising and arrogant, in that it claims to know what the public is, but defines it as no more than the mass audience; and in that it claims to know what it wants but limits its choice to the average of experience. In this sense, we reject it utterly. If there is a sense in which it should be used, it is this: what the public wants and what it has the right to get is freedom to

choose from the widest range of programme matter. Anything less than that is deprivation.[23]

And programme deprivation is most certainly a form of censorship – even if only by omission.

Following a similar line to the Report, it has been claimed with increasing frequency that 'giving people what they want' simply encourages the pursuit of the lowest common denominator – the British popular press being frequently cited as furnishing a particularly glaring example of this tendency. Nor does it necessarily introduce more freedom of choice in any meaningful sense, that is, in the sense of increasing real diversity and variety of media products. Indeed, it can convincingly be argued that unrestrained market competition tends in fact to work strongly against the choices of certain citizens, especially the poor and minorities of one kind or another, and against the best interests of all citizens to the extent that it fails to produce an adequate amount of educational, political and cultural material. This is because markets tend to work well to allocate private goods and services (cars or holidays for example) but far less well in the case of public ones such as health and education, which is why European governments have made these a matter of state provision. In broadcasting in particular, a focus purely on economic efficiency (in other words, profit maximisation) may well produce what many people want much of the time, but it frequently fails to produce what many people want some of the time, and some people want all of the time – not to mention what everybody needs in their role as citizens. Certain types of broadcasting, such as documentaries, cultural programmes or even simply indigenous programmes, can be seen as what economists inimitably like to call 'merit goods' – that is, services like education or health provision, which are socially beneficial and worthwhile but which people, if simply left to their own devices, may partake of less than is in their own best interests.

Thus European governments have put in place structures which protect and indeed encourage certain types of broadcast content, which are seen as collectively desirable and of benefit to people as citizens but which they might not always watch in large enough numbers to make their existence viable in purely economic terms.[24]

In Britain, the effects of 'deregulation' on public service broadcasting have been extremely destructive. For example, reducing ITV's pubic service obligations in the 1990s and forcing it to compete with the purely commercial broadcaster BSkyB led almost immediately to the ditching of its flagship current affairs programmes *World in Action* and *This Week*, and for a while even the venerable *News at Ten* was shuffled around in the schedules to make way for movies at nine o'clock. As well as reducing its local news provision, ITV now makes no programmes for children, and many of the children's channels provided by BSkyB consist entirely of programmes imported from the US. In 1999 a report written by Steven Barnett and Emily Seymour for the Campaign for Quality Television, and based on both content analysis and interviews with those working in television, concluded that foreign coverage had virtually disappeared from commercial television, that the BBC had become almost the sole repository of political and economic coverage of current affairs, and that across the whole system there was an overwhelming sense in both drama and current affairs that:

> The agenda is being progressively narrowed, and increasingly it is only the safe, formulaic and proven approaches that will get on screen ... The pressure on ratings – on the BBC as well as commercial television – means less scope for risk taking and commissioners who no longer believe in or cannot afford 'the right to fail'.[25]

In the current situation, there is a real risk that the BBC will end up as the only public service broadcaster, as ITV (and possibly even Channel 4) will no longer be able to afford to fulfil their public service remit, and the 'light touch' communications regulator Ofcom will not require them to do so. But as Barnett and Seymour imply, the BBC is by no means immune to these commercial pressures: in order to justify the licence fee (which successive 'deregulatory' governments have refused to increase to adequate levels, and which has been the object of incessant criticism in newspapers owned by Murdoch, whose BSkyB is of course a major competitor with the BBC) the Corporation is forced to maintain a high audience share and thus, to some extent, to compete with the commercial broadcasters on their own terms.

Further evidence for a decline in certain kinds of programming since the beginnings of 'deregulation', and thus for a reduction in choice and diversity in British broadcasting, is provided by a report compiled for the Third World and Environment Broadcasting Project which showed that

> The amount of factual international programming on the four largest terrestrial channels was 40 per cent lower in 2003 than in 1989–90 … The decline began in the early 1990s and, although levels of total output have remained fairly consistent since then, the *type* of coverage offered to viewers has changed. Increasingly prominent within factual international programming are genres that reveal little about the realities of life for non-British people living outside this country: travel programmes; series following British adventurers; documentaries about 'Brits abroad' and reality game shows in 'exotic' locations. These programmes foreground British subjects, albeit in foreign locations. Factual programming about developing countries fell even more markedly. In 2003 it was 49 per cent lower than in 1989–90 on all terrestrial tv, lower than at any other time recorded since 1989–90.[26]

Market censorship

The conclusion to which the foregoing considerations inevitably lead is that there is no reason to trust business any more than government when it comes to safeguarding freedom of expression, public debate and the integrity of the media. Market forces may act as a less overt form of censorship than state-imposed cuts and bans, but to the extent that they limit the production of certain forms of content – either because they are not profitable, displease the advertisers, or conflict with the proprietors' other interests – they can perfectly properly be regarded as censors. As John Keane has argued, those concerned with freedom of expression today must above all recognise that:

> Communications markets restrict freedom of communication by generating barriers to entry, monopoly and restrictions upon choice, and by shifting the prevailing definition of information from that of a public good to a privately appropriable commodity. In short, it must be concluded that there is a structural contradiction between freedom of communication and unlimited freedom of the market, and that the market liberal ideology of freedom of individual choice in the marketplace of opinions is in fact a justification for the privileging of corporate speech and of giving more choice to investors than to citizens. It is an apology for the power of king-sized business to organise and determine and therefore to *censor* individuals' choices concerning what they listen to or read and watch.[27]

Market competition thus produces market censorship. Those who control the media marketplace ultimately determine what media contents are produced and thus which ideas gain entry into the 'marketplace of opinions'. As Dallas Smythe has argued:

> The act of modern censorship is essentially a decision as to what is to be mass produced in the cultural area. So long as current

cultural production is in the hands of privately owned giant corporations, *they* must also make decisions as to what is to be mass produced in the cultural area and what will not be produced. Because in monopoly capitalism, privately owned giant corporations are regarded as legal persons, we are accustomed to yield them the same privileges to which natural persons are entitled. *It is as accurate therefore to refer to corporate decision making in the cultural area as being censorship as it is to refer to government decision making by that pejorative term.*[28]

In order to try to illustrate how these processes work out in practice, let us turn finally to the workings of the media empires of Rupert Murdoch and Silvio Berlusconi.

'A politico-business model'

When Murdoch acquired his first British newspaper, the *News of the World*, in 1969, he wanted, according to its then editor Stafford Somerfield, 'to read proofs, write a leader if he felt like it, change the paper around and give instructions to staff'. Remonstrations were met with the curt response 'I didn't come all this way not to interfere'. Somerfield did not last long, nor did a subsequent editor, Barry Askew, who complained that Murdoch 'would come into the office and literally re-write leaders which were not supporting the hard Thatcher monetarist line. That were not, in fact, supporting – slavishly – the Tory government'.[29] Over at the *Sun*, meanwhile, Murdoch changed the paper's allegiance from Labour to Tory (in spite of the fact that the majority of its readers were Labour voters) in time for the 1974 General Election. In 1981 he acquired *The Times* and the *Sunday Times* in a deal which should have been referred to the Monopolies and Mergers Commission but which wasn't, thanks to the Faustian pact which he had struck with

Margaret Thatcher, whereby her government would support his business interests and his newspapers would act as its cheerleaders.[30] Having thus acquired the *Sunday Times* he proceeded to make his hostility to the latter's liberal editor, Frank Giles, abundantly clear. According to Giles he would spread the paper out before him and demand 'what do you want to print rubbish like that for? or, pointing to a particular by-line, snarl "that man's a commie"'.[31] Giles's days at the paper were severely numbered.

Meanwhile, at *The Times*, Murdoch was telling its veteran home affairs editor Fred Emery that 'I give instructions to my editors all around the world, why shouldn't I in London?'. This remark is reported in *Good Times, Bad Times*, by Harry Evans, who edited the pre-Murdoch *Sunday Times* and *The Times* for a year under the new proprietor, a year which he describes as distinctly unpleasant. As he puts it in this seminal text on the Murdoch style:

> The aura he created in 1981–2 was one of bleak hostility to Edward Heath and the Tory rebels, and contempt for the Social Democrats. He did this by persistent derision of them at our meetings and on the telephone, by sending me articles marked 'worth reading!' which espoused right-wing views, by jabbing a finger at headlines which he thought could have been more supportive of Mrs Thatcher.[32]

According to Evans, Murdoch objected to the balanced assessment of the government which the paper was presenting, and called for more 'conviction' (ibid.),[33] which Evans took to mean cheerleading. The paper's warning that the unemployment figures were reaching three million were met with the response that *The Times* should be writing about the numbers of people employed, particularly in comparison with Europe (long a particular Murdoch hate object). As Evans concludes:

None of this represented a reasonable exchange of views between editor and proprietor, unexceptional on any newspaper. The tone was assertive and hostile to debate. Such incidents were not isolated. They amounted to pressures to manipulate the independent editorial policy of *The Times* and they escalated into a campaign.[34]

Giles was replaced at the *Sunday Times* by Andrew Neil, a man very much in the Murdoch mould, but when this mutually beneficial relationship eventually came unstuck Neil published a memoir which is a key text not simply on the Murdoch modus operandi but on that of the modern media baron in general. In particular, he pinpoints how the owner allocates a good deal of control over the day-to-day running of his papers to like-minded editors and managers. However, as Neil notes, in the Murdoch empire, editorial freedom has its limits, because 'Rupert has an uncanny knack of being there even when he is not'[35] because his staff try to second-guess what he would want, even in the most unimportant of matters. This modus operandi is also very well summed up by Murdoch's former right hand man in China, Bruce Dover:

> The thing about Murdoch is that he very rarely issued directives or instructions to his senior executives or editors. Instead, by way of discussion he would make known his personal viewpoint on a certain matter. What was expected in return, at least from those seeking tenure of any length in the Murdoch Empire, was a sort of 'anticipatory compliance'. One didn't need to be instructed about what to do, one simply knew what was in one's long-term interests.[36]

Thus it was that Murdoch's world-view, neatly summed up by Neil as 'a combination of right-wing Republicanism from America mixed with undiluted Thatcherism from Britain and stirred in with some anti-British Establishment sentiments as befits his colonial heritage',[37] was able so thoroughly to infuse his newspapers without the constant need for direct intervention.

That all this resulted in various forms of censorship, both direct and indirect, is undeniable. Claire Tomalin, the former literary editor of the *Sunday Times*, has spoken of a 'reign of terror'; Peter Wilby, the paper's former education correspondent, remembers 'a tone of fear, a horrible, "totalitarian" atmosphere'; and the renowned Latin American specialist Isabel Hilton has stated that:

> The sense of intimidation was so strong that people actually started censoring themselves because it is very unpleasant to get into this kind of argument all the time. It is not just a collection of incidents, it's a collection of incidents *and* the atmosphere, which in the end is so depressing. You stop functioning as a journalist. There are things you just don't bother to pursue because you know you just won't get them into the paper.[38]

Nor is Murdoch's autocratic attitude towards his papers confined only to his British ones. In the 1970s he insisted that his *New York Post* support Ed Koch over Mario Cuomo in the campaign for Mayor of New York. When eighty of its reporters signed a petition which stated that 'we are dismayed to be manipulated into mere pamphleteers' and argued that the *Post* was their paper too, Murdoch replied: 'Oh no it's not. When you pay the losses you can say it's your paper. It's my newspaper. You just work here, and don't you forget it'[39]. Meanwhile, in his native, Australia Murdoch is notorious for having shifted around his newspapers' political allegiances in order to back whichever party he judges at the time will be the most friendly to his media interests. During the 1975 election campaign, for instance, Murdoch was in one of his anti-Labour phases and his paper the *Australian*, which had previously been pro-Labour, became so overtly hostile that seventy-five of its journalists signed a letter complaining that the paper had been turned into a propaganda sheet and protesting at

> the deliberate or careless slanting of headlines, seemingly blatant imbalance in news presentation and political censorship. Also on occasion the distortion of copy from senior, specialist journalists, the political management of news and features and the stifling of dissident and even unpalatable impartial opinion in the paper's columns.[40]

In 1994 the *Sunday Times* ran a number of articles investigating possible links between British aid to Malaysia to enable it to build the Pergau dam, and a vast Malaysian arms contract placed with Britain. These revelations of arms-for-aid infuriated the Malaysian Prime Minister, Mahathir Mohamed, and provoked a furious phone call to Murdoch, who shouted at Neil: 'You're boring people! You're doing far too much on Malaysia. Page after page of it, which nobody can understand. Malaysia doesn't merit all this coverage ... It's my fault, I've been letting you get on with it. But it's too much, it has to stop'.[41] Shortly thereafter, Neil left the *Sunday Times*. The following year, a British minister dining with the British High Commissioner in Kuala Lumpur asked if the Malaysian government was still as hostile to British business interests as it had appeared to be in the wake of the Pergau revelations. The High Commissioner replied: 'Not since Murdoch fixed it with Mahathir. The Malaysian Prime Minister made it clear that Murdoch would never do business in his country as long as Andrew Neil was editor of the *Sunday Times*'.[42] Later, another British minister was told by Mahathir himself that when he protested to Murdoch about the articles the latter told him that he had a 'rogue editor' on his hands but that the matter was being 'sorted out'.[43]

The 'business' about which Murdoch was so concerned was of course the expansion of his satellite television interests into South East Asia, and especially into the vast market of China.

On 1 September 1992, Murdoch, in full-on evangelising mode, had made the cataclysmic error of declaiming in a speech at London's Banqueting House:

> Advances in the technology of telecommunications have proved an unambiguous threat to totalitarian regimes everywhere. Fax machines enable dissidents to bypass state-controlled print media. Direct-dial telephony makes it difficult for a state to control interpersonal voice communications. And satellite broadcasting makes it possible for information-hungry residents of many closed societies to bypass state controlled television channels.[44]

Absolutely nothing could have been guaranteed to displease China's leaders more, and all of Murdoch's subsequent acts of censorship regarding China can be seen as attempts to establish himself in their eyes as a business partner as compliant as the Western Internet companies discussed in chapter 5. Hence, for example, one of his first acts in 1994 on acquiring the STAR TV satellite service, whose signal could be picked up in parts of China, was to drop the BBC, some of whose programmes had offended the Chinese government. Amongst the many who criticised the move was the Governor of Hong Kong, Chris Patten, who called it 'the most seedy of betrayals'.[45] Then in 1998 the East Asia editor of *The Times*, Jonathan Mirsky, whose critical comments on the regime had caused his visa to be revoked, forcing him to work from Hong Kong, resigned his post on the grounds that in recent times ninety per cent of the articles on China which he had submitted to the paper had not been published, and that on this subject he sensed the heavy hand of Murdoch all over the paper. And when in 1997 Murdoch discovered that one of his companies, HarperCollins, was publishing the memoirs of Chris Patten, which were not exactly complimentary to the Chinese leadership, he demanded that the book be dumped. The official reason given was that 'the material as it stands does not match up to the original outline or indeed inspire us from a commercial standpoint',[46] but newspapers (apart from those owned by Murdoch) were not blind to the real reason for this act of censorship, the *New York Times* calling it 'contemptible', the *Daily Telegraph* referring to Murdoch as 'the biggest gangster of them all', and the *Financial Times* noting that 'we glimpse this modern master of the capitalist universe bent double before the potentates of the people in Beijing'.[47] That Murdoch was more than willing to tailor his media's content to the requirements of the Chinese authorities in order to be granted entry to the lucrative Chinese market, is clear from a speech which he made in Tokyo on 15 May 1997 in which he stated that:

> Advances in telecommunications contribute to the 'universalisation' of cultural interests and lifestyles. However, nations retain their own social and moral values that the media must take into account. China is a distinctive market with distinctive social and moral values that Western companies must learn to abide by.[48]

Even more forthright in this respect was a speech which he gave to – of all things! – the Party School of the China Communist Party Central Committee on 8 October 2003 in which he assured the assembled Politburo members that:

> The potential of the open market doesn't represent any loss of power. China has the potential not only to follow the examples of the US and the UK, but to improve upon those examples and achieve a level of success of its own. By developing a regulatory system that is both firm enough to ensure China's control over her emerging businesses and smart enough not to stifle those businesses' growth, China will create an exemplary media industry.[49]

The contrast with the buccaneering Banqueting House speech simply could not be more marked, and the fact that Murdoch's tactics of cajoling and manipulation, which in part involved trading media freedom for market entry, ultimately failed when it came to the Chinese leadership, makes them no less egregious.

Murdoch's dealings with the Chinese, even though ultimately unsuccessful from his point of view, illustrate particularly clearly the thesis advanced by Bruce Page, a former leading journalist on *The Sunday Times*, that Murdoch's media activities need to be understood in terms of a 'politico-business model'[50] and that Newscorp is about eroding the boundaries between state power and media operations. In particular he argues (with a wealth of examples) that Newscorp's core competence consists in 'swapping approval with the controllers of the state'.[51] In this vision of things, the function of journalism is not to act as a watchdog but, on the contrary, to maintain sympathetic relations with authority.

The reason for such comprehensive abandonment of the ideals of the Fourth Estate can be summed up in two words: self interest. Murdoch routinely uses his media to support governments which support his business interests. So, for example, Murdoch's papers' vociferous support for Thatcher meant that Sky's highly irregular takeover of its rival BSB in November 1990 was never referred to the regulatory authorities, and that the resulting venture, BSkyB, was allowed to operate with almost none of the public service requirements which attach to its rivals, the terrestrial broadcasters. In the mid-1990s the Labour Party in the UK let it be known that it would drop its traditional hostility to Murdoch's expansionism, and thus, in the 1997 and 2001 General Elections, the *Sun* supported Labour. Murdoch was then handsomely repaid in the Communications Act 2003, which enabled him finally to make significant inroads into British terrestrial television. Then, during the invasion of

Iraq, the Murdoch press not only acted as a cheerleader for Blair but savagely attacked as 'disloyal' any media outlet – especially the hated BBC – daring to voice criticism of the war. (Significantly, not one of the newspapers owned by Murdoch anywhere in the world opposed the war.) The corollary of this kind of mutual back-scratching is, of course, a ferocious hostility to governments, political parties and indeed any institutions which Murdoch deems inimical to his business interests – witness his Australian papers' pivotal role in the destabilisation of the Gough Whitlam government in 1974–5; and, in Britain, the remorseless hostility of his papers towards pre-Blair Labour, the government of John Major (which had the temerity to suggest that the cross-media ownership regulations needed tightening); and the European Union (which Murdoch has always regarded as a block to the expansion of his media empire).

Such a conception of the role of the media certainly results in censorship, since voices, viewpoints and stories which don't 'fit' simply remain unheard, or else are demonised out of all recognition. It also results in the otherwise incomprehensible spectacle of one medium calling for the censorship of another, the most spectacular example of which was the ferocious campaign by the *Sunday Times* in 1988 against the ITV documentary *Death on the Rock*, which had the audacity to question the official account of the shooting dead by British soldiers of three IRA members in Gibraltar.[52] In his memoir *Full Disclosure*, *Sunday Times* former editor Andrew Neil states that 'on many of the biggest issues of the day, the *Sunday Times* stood shoulder to shoulder' with Margaret Thatcher, and that 'Thatcher's battles were our battles',[53] and it is extremely disturbing that these included her battles to bully and browbeat into submission the terrestrial broadcasters and the Independent Broadcasting Authority (the then regulator of ITV and Channel 4).

Bruce Page concludes that the positioning of Murdoch's papers, in whatever country they are based, is motivated above all by corporate tactics, and that this leaves an indelible stain on the journalism within them. The result is the publication of what he calls 'pseudo-newspapers',[54] and, at worst, a pernicious form of 'anti-journalism'[55] and 'privatised government propaganda',[56] in which censorship by both omission and distortion play equally key roles.

Depressing and worrying though this spectacle may be, however, it pales into relative insignificance when compared with what has been happening to the media in Italy since the early 1980s.

Sua Emittenza

In the 1980s the building magnate Silvio Berlusconi established three commercial television networks, Canale 5, Rete 4 and Italia 1, in effect a monopoly of commercial television under the control of his company Mediaset, in clear breach of the Italian constitution. That he was originally able to do this was thanks to the patronage of Bettino Craxi, then leader of the Italian Socialist Party. Needless to say, coverage of Craxi and his party on the Mediaset channels was not exactly unsympathetic. However, even after Craxi's departure in 1987 Berlusconi managed to sabotage all attempts to remedy this situation. Indeed, in 1990, the Italian parliament passed a law which stated that no one individual could own more than three national networks, thereby legitimising what by then had simply become the status quo.

By 1983, Berlusconi's channels were achieving higher ratings than those of the public broadcaster Radiotelevisione Italiana (RAI). And just like Murdoch, Berlusconi sold his channels to advertisers and audiences alike on the back of a populist appeal to freedom. As Alexander Stille puts it:

He managed to convey the feeling that he was not just selling a product, but offering a vision of a new, better world, offering a message of empowerment and liberation for small businesses that had been unable to break through into the big time; he offered a kind of utopian vision of infinite growth and infinite prosperity and well-being. Berlusconi is not wrong when he describes himself as a 'missionary' of commercial television.[57]

By the following year, RAI, which is only part-funded by a licence fee, was showing 46,080 advertisements totalling 311 hours, and the Mediaset channels a staggering 494,000 advertisements totalling 3,468 hours. Fifty-three per cent of all Italian advertising budgets are spent on television, and by 2003 Mediaset was responsible for over sixty per cent of the entire television advertising market.

No wonder, then, that Berlusconi rapidly acquired the nickname *Sua Emittenza* – His Broadcastingship.

Inevitably RAI ended up aping Mediaset and competing with it exclusively on its own terms – undemanding entertainment in pursuit of high ratings. As Paul Ginsborg put it: 'A grotesque duopoly was created: on the one side a flagging public broadcasting system, on the other the suffocating pre-eminence of Berlusconi's three channels. The combination produced a deeply conformist, repetitive and uncritically consumer-oriented television system',[58] in which diverse and demanding content was increasingly conspicuous by its absence. In other words, what has been called the 'savage deregulation' of Italian television produced a particularly acute form of market censorship.

But worse was to come. By the early 1990s, the two largest Italian political parties, the Christian Democrats and the Socialists, had been totally wiped out as a consequence of both the investigations into political corruption known as the *Mani Pulite* (Clean Hands) and the emergence of the separatist Northern League. It was thus expected that the next elections would be won by the Democratic Party of the Left and their allies in the Progressive coalition. Well aware that the Left was hostile to his media empire, Berlusconi formed the political movement Forza Italia (whose name echoes the football chant 'Come on, Italy!') in 1993 and on 26 January 1994 announced he was contesting the forthcoming elections. Indeed, the way in which Berlusconi sold his politics was a mirror image of the way in which he had sold commercial television. As Stille points out, it consisted of

> a call to arms of the Italian middle class against the asphyxiating oppression of the old political parties, represented by the monopoly of state broadcasting, against the cultural and economic elites that dominated the country and for the promise of liberation and the land of milk and honey.[59]

Forming alliances with the Northern League and the 'post-fascist' National Alliance, he immediately launched a massive electoral campaign on the Mediaset channels – and not simply in the advertising slots. At one point, Raimondo Vianello, the presenter of *Pressing*, Italia 1's top sports show, announced on air his backing for Berlusconi; at another, a young would-be starlet, Ambra Angiolini, proclaimed during a show featuring thirteen-year-old dancers that 'God is rooting for Berlusconi, while the Devil, we know, is rooting for Occhetto' [the leader of the Left].[60] On Rete 4, the presenter Emilio Fede, who is also the channel's news director and who has been nicknamed 'Fido' because of his faithfulness to his boss, cancelled the normal afternoon schedule on 6 February 1994 and broadcast the entirety of a Berlusconi speech, from the rousing applause at its commencement to the equally rousing applause at its end. Official monitoring of broadcast election coverage showed that Rete 4 devoted sixty-eight percent of its coverage to Berlusconi and Forza Italia and seventy-seven percent to the coalition of which it was the key member. Similarly, research conducted by the University of Rome demonstrated that on the Berlusconi networks, 37.5% of coverage of Forza Italia was favourable, whilst 41.2% of coverage of the Left was negative.

Berlusconi won the elections, with Forza Italia gaining twenty-one per cent of the vote, the highest percentage of any single party. As Alexander Stille concludes:

> Even if the principal effect of Berlusconi's TV was in creating a general cultural-political disposition that was favourable to him, his unusual access to television during the campaign cannot be dismissed as an unimportant contributing factor. Berlusconi's campaign is simply inconceivable without his television networks. Being able to immediately reach half the households in Italy whenever he wanted is something no other candidate enjoyed.[61]

Berlusconi was appointed Prime Minister, but his term in office failed to last the year, mainly because of the inherent contradictions in his coalition. However, in 2001 Berlusconi again became Prime Minister, this time as leader of the centre-right coalition House of Freedoms, which once again included Forza Italia, the National Alliance, the Northern League and some small centrist parties. In spite of the inevitable conflicts within the coalition, Berlusconi managed to stay in power until the 2006 elections, when he was narrowly defeated by the centre-left coalition led by Romano Prodi. This collapsed in January 2008. In February, Berlusconi announced the formation of the 'People of Freedom', a new party/coalition in which the National Alliance and Forza Italia merged, fighting and winning the elections held in April.

As Tobias Jones argues: 'Having a politician who owns three television channels turns any election into the equivalent of a football match in which one team kicks-off with a three-goal advantage'.[62] But, in his periods as Prime Minister, Berlusconi has also controlled RAI as well, thus being responsible for ninety per cent of Italian television viewership. But 'responsible' is hardly the word to describe how he has used this extraordinary fusion of media and political power. For example, on his early evening news programme Emilio Fede once stated on Rete 4, 'to me Berlusconi is eternal' and followed this up with 'I love Silvio Berlusconi'. As Paul Statham puts it:

> It is not only the personal ownership of the means of public communication by Berlusconi that has been seen as a threat to pluralism, but also the willingness of his television networks to employ communication strategies that break the traditional norms and practices of independent public broadcasting, which are designed to ensure a degree of political objectivity. The television news channels on Berlusconi's networks select versions of events that are explicitly favourable to Berlusconi personally and to Forza Italia. On the news programmes of Retequattro and Italia Uno, the presenters intervene to explain the news, explicitly defending statements made by Berlusconi and attacking those of his adversaries. The television news often finishes with staged interviews with people on the street who offer eulogies to Berlusconi and denigrate his opponents, or the news concludes with unscientific opinion polls that give much higher ratings to Forza Italia than independent sources. The image and voice of Silvio Berlusconi are omnipresent, but in a controlled and stylised format usually recorded on video. Feature films are interrupted to bring news of his latest speech, and subliminal advertising techniques have been used to communicate political messages in non-political television programmes. Popular celebrities extol the virtues of Forza Italia on mainstream talk shows and other programmes, such as the *Wheel of Fortune* game show. Vittorio Sgarbi and Giuliano Ferrara, established political commentators with long-standing programmes on Berlusconi networks, both used their programmes to promote Berlusconi and Forza Italia. They

then assumed key state positions on media and culture in his government.[63]

In 2002 Daniele Luttazzi, Michele Santoro and Enzo Biagi were dismissed from RAI after Berlusconi had very publicly accused them of being 'criminal' in their use of state channels. During the election period in the previous year, Luttazi, the host of the satirical talk-show *Satyricon*, had interviewed Marco Travaglio, the author of a book which explored the origins of Berlusconi's wealth. Santoro had done likewise on his programme *Sciuscià*. In the same period, the veteran journalist Biagi had, on his programme *Il Fatto*, interviewed the comic actor Roberto Benigni, who had ridiculed Berlusconi in no uncertain terms. Subsequently both *Sciuscià* and *Il Fatto* were not recommissioned. By the end of April, new directors of the RAI channels had been appointed. Admittedly RAI had always been carved up by main political parties (in a process known as *lottizzazione* or 'sharing out'), and this continued under Berlusconi. Thus RAI 3 remained in the hands of the Left, but RAI 1 was headed by Fabrizio del Noce, a Forza Italia stalwart, and RAI 2 by Antonio Marano of the Northern League. The news programmes on these channels were now headed by Clemente Mimun (Forza Italia) and Mauro Mazza (National Alliance). Thereafter, the claims of political interference and connivance continued unabated. For example, in February 2003 RAI refused to provide live coverage of a huge demonstration in Rome against the Iraq war (of which Berlusconi was a supporter), and in the following November Mediaset filed a suit for defamation against the first episode of RAI's new satirical show *RaiOt*, causing the remaining five episodes to be pulled.

As John Carlin put it in the *Observer* 18 January 2004:

> To say that Berlusconi, who is the richest man in Italy … has crossed the line between big business and politics would be a ludicrous understatement. Never in history – at least not in the

history of Western democracy – has anything like it ever been seen. It's as if Rupert Murdoch were president of the US, but in addition to owning Fox he also owned CBS and NBC. But Berlusconi, in the Italian context, is actually more than that. He is a mix of Murdoch and Bill Gates, laced with a generous measure of Mohamed Al Fayed. Berlusconi – or, in some cases, his wife and children – owns virtually all of Italy's commercial TV networks, the country's biggest advertising company, the biggest publishing house, the biggest film distribution business, two national newspapers, 50 magazines and internet service providers. He is a big player in the construction business and insurance, and he is president of Italy's most glamorous football club, current European champions AC Milan. On top of all that, as head of a political party that he – or rather his advertising company, Publitalia – created in two months in 1994, he has been elected prime minister of Italy twice.

This quite extraordinary situation, which raises the most serious concerns about the plurality and independence of the media in Italy, and which clearly gives rise to various forms of both direct and indirect censorship, has been the subject of critical resolutions in the European Parliament and the Council of Europe, and has been attacked by the Organisation for Security and Co-operation in Europe (OSCE), Reporters Without Borders, the International Federation of Journalists and many others. One of its most trenchant critics has been the UK's *Economist* magazine, which has repeatedly pointed out that the charge sheet against Berlusconi includes not simply staggering conflicts of interest and the gross abuse of media power but money laundering, complicity in murder, connections with the Mafia, tax evasion, and bribing politicians, judges and the tax police. On 28 April 2001 it pronounced that 'Mr Berlusconi is not fit to lead the government of any country, least of all one of the world's richest democracies' and on 2 August 2003 it condemned his behaviour as 'an outrage against the Italian people and their judicial system' and 'Europe's most extreme example of the abuse by a capitalist of the democracy within which he lives and operates'.

The arguments for Berlusconi as censor, then, are that he has greatly narrowed the range of programming available on all Italian television, debasing vast tracts of it to the level of *panem et circenses* (bread and circuses). Indeed, Tobias Jones has called it 'the worst, most abysmal television on the planet'.[64] Its contents may indeed be popular with some sections of the audience, but it has also served to narrow the choices of other sections and to deny everyone their full communicative rights. In political terms he has used his Mediaset channels consistently to extol Forza Italia whilst excluding or excoriating his political opponents, and, during his periods as Prime Minister, attempted to neuter RAI both politically and commercially. More generally, he stands accused of narrowing, trivialising and commodifying all political discourse on Italian television. If all that doesn't amount to a poisonous combination of both political and economic censorship, the word is entirely meaningless.

Conclusion: censorship and freedom of expression

Two of the main themes of this book are that censorship is still alive and well today, and that it exists in democratic societies as well as in authoritarian ones. Of course, the mechanisms by which censorship operates today vary greatly from society to society. For example, in America, market censorship is more developed than it is in the UK (although it is most certainly making inroads there too). On the other hand, freedom of expression in the US has been powerfully shielded by the First Amendment, whereas in the UK a statutory right to freedom of expression was established only with the passing of the Human Rights Act 1998 (see below), and governments quite clearly regard it as perfectly right and proper that they exercise a degree of control over media content (particularly in the spheres of 'taste and decency'), which Americans (and, for that matter, most other Europeans) would find unacceptable. Meanwhile, in the wake of 9/11 and the subsequent 'war on terror', both governments have used the spectre of terrorism to attempt to legitimise measures which, among other things, restrict freedom of expression: for example, in the US the Patriot Act 2001 (which creates an extremely broad definition of 'domestic terrorism', which may well exert a chilling effect on free

expression and association); and in the UK the Serious
Organised Crime and Police Act 2005 (which greatly extends
police powers to control protests and demonstrations) and the
Terrorism Act 2006 (which makes the 'encouragement of
terrorism' a worryingly broad and vague offence).

An indivisible principle

Underlying this book has been the presumption, largely taken
for granted in the US, but nothing like as well established in the
UK (except at a largely rhetorical level), that freedom of expression is a Good Thing. This is not a particularly fashionable point
of view these days, even, or perhaps in particular, with the
otherwise liberal-minded. As Ronald Dworkin has pointed out,
in recent times, freedom of expression has been attacked not just
by governments but also by

> new enemies who claim to speak for justice not tyranny, and
> who point to other values we respect, including self-determi-
> nation, equality and freedom from racial hatred and prejudice,
> as reasons why the right of free speech should now be demoted
> to a much lower grade of urgency and importance.[1]

This view has also found sympathy with those worried about
what they regard as the imposition of Western values on non-
Western cultures. The fundamental problem, however, is that
either freedom of speech is a basic principle – and thus indivisible – or it is not a principle at all. To quote Dworkin again:

> It is tempting to think that even if some liberty of speech must
> be counted a universal right, this right cannot be absolute; that
> those whose opinions are too threatening or base or contrary to
> the moral or religious consensus have forfeited any right to the
> concern on which the right rests. But such a reservation would

destroy the principle: it would leave room only for the point-less grant of protection for ideas or tastes or prejudices that those in power approve, or in any case do not fear.[2]

In the US, the First Amendment gives such a position consider-able constitutional force. In Europe, meanwhile, the situation regarding freedom of expression appears at first sight to be very similar. Thus Article 10 (1) of the European Convention on Human Rights (ECHR) boldly states that: 'Everyone has the right to freedom of expression. This right shall include freedom to hold opinions and to receive and impart information and ideas without interference by public authority and regardless of frontiers'. We might also note a ringing judgement of the European Court of Human Rights in 1976 to the effect that:

> Freedom of expression constitutes one of the essential founda-tions of a democratic society and one of the basic conditions for its progress and for each individual's self-fulfilment. It is applic-able not only to information or ideas that are favourably received or regarded as inoffensive or as a matter of indiffer-ence, but also to those that offend, shock or disturb. Such are the demands of pluralism, tolerance and broad-mindedness without which there is no democratic society.[3]

So far so good. However Article 10 (2) of the ECHR continues:

> The exercise of these freedoms, since it carries with it duties and responsibilities, may be subject to such formalities, condi-tions, restrictions or penalties as are prescribed by law and are necessary in a democratic society, in the interests of national security, territorial integrity or public safety, for the prevention of disorder or crime, for the protection of health or morals, for the protection of the reputation or the rights of others, for preventing the disclosure of information received in

confidence, or for maintaining the authority and impartiality of the judiciary.

One of the main problems in Britain is that judges have tended in cases involving freedom of expression to try to strike a balance between Articles 10 (1) and 10 (2). This may be partly because they are still getting used to a rights-based jurisprudence, since the ECHR was incorporated into British law only in 1998 by the Human Rights Act. However, as Robertson and Nicol point out, Article 10 does not actually require a balancing act between free speech and other values of equal weight. Quoting the judgement of the European Court in a 1979 case, which held that Article 10 (2) should be regarded as containing 'a number of exceptions which must be strictly construed and narrowly interpreted and convincingly established', they argue that:

> Once the Court is satisfied that there has been an infringement [of Article 10 (1)], the burden shifts to the Government or to the party seeking to justify the breach to prove that the infringing law is a clearly defined restriction which legitimately serves an Article 10 (2) value and its application is necessary – not expedient – to serve a pressing social need in a democratic society, and is a reasonably proportionate response to that need. In short, the Act writes into British law, for the first time, a presumption in favour of free speech, putting the burden on the censor to justify, as a matter of necessity and of logic, the restriction imposed.[4]

But if British courts have been slow to acknowledge this fact, there have also been problems at the level of the European Court itself, caused by Article 10 (2) clearly allowing individual states a certain 'margin of appreciation' when assessing the need for interfering with freedom of expression. As Robertson and Nicol explain, this margin is 'the latitude which an international court allows to nation states to bend human rights rules in the supposed interests of its own cultural values and traditions. Decisions that turn on the "margin of appreciation" are to that extent cop-outs, and the Strasbourg court has been particularly prone to cop-out on questions of morality'.[5] Indeed, in this respect the Court has been far too prone to fall back upon an earlier judgement which argued that:

> It is not possible to find in the domestic law of the various Contracting States a uniform conception of morals. The view taken by their respective laws of the requirements of morals varies from time to time and from place to place, especially in our era which is characterised by a rapid and far-reaching evolution of opinions on the subject.[6]

But whilst no-one would want to argue for the imposition of a homogenous 'Euro morality', nor would it be desirable if 'margins of appreciation' were granted to individual European states which were so wide as to render Article 10's underlying principle largely impotent and vacuous.

Without wishing for a single moment to underestimate the importance of Article 10 to freedom of expression, particularly in a Britain which until recently lacked a statutory right to any such thing, it has to be admitted that the much more unequivocal First Amendment is a far more effective weapon against censorship. However, just how very far removed are British attitudes from American ones on this matter is graphically illustrated by the telling remark by the Labour MP Derek Wyatt to the effect that: 'We recently went to look at family online safety in Washington. Immediately the lawyers jumped up and said, "No, we have the First Amendment. We have got to allow pornography". I said, "No, if it is the First Amendment, you can amend it. That is what you do in a democracy"'.[7]

Hate speech

Even the First Amendment, however, recognises that the right to freedom of expression is not absolute, and rights-based jurisprudence recognises equally that certain rights have to be balanced against others. In this respect it's important to realise that Article 20 (2) of the International Covenant on Civil and Political Rights states that any advocacy of national, racial or religious hatred that constitutes incitement to discrimination, hostility or violence shall be prohibited by law. This obviously has consequences for freedom of expression. But the Covenant allows this freedom to be limited in the name of prohibiting the incitement of hatred only if there is a close nexus between the expression in question and the risk of harm, and when the risk is imminent. Conscious intent must be proved and the anticipated danger cannot be merely hypothetical or conjectural.

Such considerations quite rightly place the bar extremely high when it comes to justifying censorship. But by no means impossibly high. For example, during the genocide of 1993–4 in Rwanda, Radio Télévision Libre de Mille Collines, a privately owned radio station, regularly broadcast clear incitements to violence against the Tutsis and moderate Hutus. After the shooting down of President Habyarimana's plane, which precipitated the genocide, it called for a 'final war' to 'exterminate the cockroaches', and during the genocide itself it broadcast lists of people to be killed and even instructed people where to find them. After the genocide, the International Criminal Tribunal for Rwanda found the radio's top executives Jean-Bosco Barayagwiza and Ferdinand Nahimana guilty of genocide, incitement to genocide and crimes against humanity. They were sentenced to imprisonment for thirty-five years and for life respectively.

In Britain, expression may legally be regulated in the interests of the freedom of others to go about their business in public without being assaulted or defamed, and may be curtailed in order to avoid public disorder which may follow the provocative dissemination of racist ideas. It is also an offence to possess racially inflammatory material with a view to publication in circumstances where racial hatred is likely to be stirred up. In the US, however, only words which 'by their very utterance inflict injury or tend to incite an *immediate* breach of the peace' (emphasis added) are denied protection under the First Amendment. This is very much in line with Justice Louis Brandeis' famous judgement in *Whitney v California* in 1927:

> Fear of serious injury cannot alone justify suppression of free speech and assembly. Men feared witches and burnt women. It is the function of speech to free men from the bondage of irrational fears. To justify suppression of free speech there must be reasonable ground to fear that serious evil will result if free speech is practiced. There must be reasonable ground to believe that the danger apprehended is imminent. There must be reasonable ground to believe that the evil to be prevented is a serious one.[8]

One of the problems of restrictions on what has come to be called 'hate speech' is that they can all too easily be used to suppress not only dissent but free expression on the part of the very minorities which they are supposed to protect. Turkey, for example, frequently uses Article 312 of the Penal Code – which provides for up to three year's imprisonment for anyone who 'incites hatred based on class, race, religion, or religious sect, or incites hatred between different regions' – against those who espouse Kurdish nationalism or even express pride in Kurdish culture. And in various Central Asian countries, hate speech laws are routinely used to censor Islamist movements, even though there is no evidence that censoring or banning such groups has any impact on their existence or rising influence. In fact, most evidence testifies to the fact that criminalising such groups all too often results in their further radicalisation. And here again we can turn to Justice Louis Brandeis, who argued that when faced with expression of which we disapprove, the solution is not censorship but engagement with the issues which it raises, and, where appropriate, post-publication chastisement (but not pre-publication censorship):

> If there be time to expose through discussion the falsehood and fallacies, to avert the evil by the processes of education, the remedy to be applied is more speech, not enforced silence … Among free men, the deterrents ordinarily to be applied to prevent crime are education and punishment for violations of the law, not abridgment of the rights of free speech and assembly.[9]

By way of illustrating this extremely important point, let us look at two different ways of dealing with a form of hate speech.

In September 1996, the historian David Irving filed a libel suit against Deborah Lipstadt and her British publisher Penguin Books for publishing a British edition of her book, *Denying the Holocaust*, in which she called Irving a Holocaust denier, falsifier and bigot, and argued that he manipulated and distorted his primary sources. Irving claimed to have been libelled on the grounds that Lipstadt had called him a Holocaust denier when in his opinion there was no Holocaust to deny, and that she had claimed that he had falsified evidence or deliberately misinter-preted it. In the course of the trial, the defence produced a vast amount of evidence which was extremely damaging to Irving's claims to be a serious historian, and, finding against him, Justice Charles Gray stated that:

> The charges which I have found to be substantially true include the charges that Irving has for his own ideological reasons persistently and deliberately misrepresented and manipulated historical evidence; that for the same reasons he has portrayed

> Hitler in an unwarrantedly favourable light, principally in
> relation to his attitude towards and responsibility for the treat-
> ment of the Jews; that he is an active Holocaust denier; that he
> is anti-Semitic and racist and that he associates with right-wing
> extremists who promote neo-Nazism.[10]

Not only did Irving lose the case, but in the light of the damning
evidence presented at the trial, several of his works which had
previously escaped serious scrutiny were brought to public
attention. Required to pay the very substantial costs of the trial,
he was declared bankrupt in 2002.

On 11 November 2005, Irving was arrested in Austria
(which is one of the fourteen countries in the world in which
Holocaust denial is a crime) and charged with 'trivialising the
Holocaust'. Although he exploited the ensuing trial to claim that
he had moderated his views on the Holocaust, on 20 February
2006 he pleaded guilty to the charge of 'trivialising, grossly
playing down and denying the Holocaust' and was sentenced to
three years' imprisonment. For many fellow Holocaust deniers,
this simply made Irving a martyr to the cause. Deborah Lipstadt
was amongst those who criticised the verdict, stating that 'I am
not happy when censorship wins, and I don't believe in winning
battles via censorship ... The way of fighting Holocaust deniers
is with history and with truth'.[11] She also argued that 'nothing is
served by having David Irving in a jail cell, except that he has
become an international news issue. Let him go home and let
him continue talking to six people in a basement. Let him fade
into obscurity where he belongs.[12]

Internalising the fatwa

On the other hand, there are those who argue that it is not only
speech which incites hatred that should be banned, but also

speech which some find simply offensive. This is an attitude which has gained considerable ground ever since the *Satanic Verses* affair discussed in chapter 1. According to Kenan Malik, this represents 'a watershed in our attitudes to freedom of expression. Rushdie's critics lost the battle – *The Satanic Verses* continues to be published. But they won the war. The argument at the heart of the anti-Rushdie case – that it is morally unacceptable to cause offence to other cultures – is now widely accepted'.[13]

There is certainly a good deal of evidence for such a proposition. One of the best examples is provided by the refusal by newspapers in the US, Canada and Britain, unlike many of their counterparts across the globe, to re-publish the cartoons from the Danish newspaper *Jyllands-Posten* which caused such a stir amongst certain sections of the Muslim world in 2005 and 2006. Whatever the motives of these newspapers, whether a desire to avoid offence or a fear of physical attack, freedom of expression indubitably came off a poor second. Also in 2005, the Birmingham Rep cancelled the run of *Bezhti* (*Dishonour*), a play by the young Sikh writer Gurpreet Kaur Bhatti which depicted sexual abuse and murder in a *gurdwara* (Sikh temple), after hundreds of Sikhs protested outside the theatre on the opening night. The following year, in order to avoid offending the many Muslims living in the area, London's Whitechapel Art Gallery removed from one of their exhibitions a number of the famous naked, life-sized dolls by the surrealist artist Hans Bellmer. In June 2007, London's Royal Court Theatre cancelled a new adaptation of Aristophanes' *Lysistrata*, set in a Muslim heaven, whilst another London theatre, the Barbican, cut parts of its production of Marlowe's *Tamburlaine the Great*, both, again, in order to avoid giving offence to Muslims.

Further evidence still is provided by the fate of Sherry Jones' novel *The Jewel of Medina*, which focuses on Muhammad's relationship with his youngest wife Aisha and which was bought by Random House in a two-book deal for $100,000 in 2007. In April 2008 the publishers sent out proofs of the book to various writers and scholars in the hope of attracting endorsements for the cover. One of these was Denise Spellberg, an associate professor of history and Middle East studies at the University of Texas whose work Jones had drawn on as a source for her novel. According to an article in the *Wall Street Journal*, 6 August 2008, Spellberg informed Shahed Amanullah, the editor of a popular Muslim website, that she had received a copy of a novel which 'made fun of Muslims and their history' and asked him to warn Muslims about it. As a result he sent a brief e-mail enquiry to a private e-mail group of graduate students involved in Middle Eastern and Islamic studies in which he stated that a professor had warned him about a forthcoming novel which she found 'incredibly offensive', asked for more information about the book, and added a write-up about it from the industry publication the *Publishers Marketplace*. The next day, a blogger, Shahid Pradhan, posted Amanullah's e-mail on a website for young Shia Muslims – Husaini Youths – under the headline 'Upcoming book, *Jewel of Medina*: a new attempt to slander the Prophet of Islam'. Shortly thereafter, another blogger, Ali Hemani, proposed a seven-point strategy to ensure 'the writer withdraws this book from the stores and apologises to all the Muslims across the world'. In the meantime, back at Random House's Knopf imprint, editor Jane Garrett had sent an e-mail to Knopf executives detailing a phone conversation with Spellberg. In it, according to Garrett, Spellberg had expressed the view that 'there is a very real possibility of major danger for the building and staff and widespread violence'. She also reported her as calling the book 'a declaration of war ... explosive stuff ... a national security issue'. She added: 'Thinks it will be far more controversial than *The Satanic Verses* and the Danish cartoons. Does not know if the author and Ballantine [another Random House imprint] folks are clueless or calculating, but thinks the book should be withdrawn ASAP'.

Shortly thereafter, Random House issued the following statement:

> After sending out advance editions of the novel *The Jewel of Medina*, we received in response, from credible and unrelated sources, cautionary advice not only that the publication of this book might be offensive to some in the Muslim community, but also that it could incite acts of violence by a small, radical segment. We felt an obligation to take these concerns very seriously. We consulted with security experts as well as with scholars of Islam, whom we asked to review the book and offer their assessments of potential reactions. We stand firmly by our responsibility to support our authors and the free discussion of ideas, even those that may be construed as offensive by some. However, a publisher must weigh that responsibility against others that it also bears, and in this instance we decided, after much deliberation, to postpone publication for the safety of the author, employees of Random House, booksellers and anyone else who would be involved in distribution and sale of the novel. The author and Ballantine subsequently agreed to terminate the agreement, with the understanding that the author would be free to publish elsewhere, if she so chose.[14]

This Jones did indeed try to do. However, her agent found that no other major publisher would touch the novel. Eventually an English publisher, Gibson Square, picked it up, but in September 2008, just days before the novel was to be published and on the twentieth anniversary of the publication of *The Satanic Verses*, their London offices were fire-bombed. Three men were arrested under the Terrorism Act 2000, two of whom pleaded guilty to the attack in April 2009. In the *Daily Telegraph*, 3 October 2008, the radical Muslim cleric Anjem Choudhary said that he was 'not surprised at all' by the attack and stated: 'It is clearly stipulated in Muslim law that any kind of attack on his honour carries the death penalty' adding: 'People should be aware of the consequences they might face when producing material like this. They should know the depth of feeling it might provoke … If the publication goes ahead then I think, inevitably, there will be more attacks like this – this is the thin end of the wedge'. The publication of the book was postponed, publisher and author each blaming the other for the decision. Nonetheless, at the time of writing the book has been published in five countries – the US, Germany, Denmark, Serbia, and Italy – with no repercussions. Plans for publication are underway in Spain, Hungary, Brazil, Russia, Macedonia, Finland and Poland, and there have also been negotiations with publishers in Sweden and The Netherlands.

Writing in his blog in *The New York Times*, Stanley Fish argued that 'Random House is free to publish or decline to publish whatever it likes, and its decision to do either has nothing whatsoever to do with the Western tradition of free speech or any other high-sounding abstraction'. In Fish's view, censorship occurs only when governments criminalise expression, and when the restrictions thus imposed are blanket ones. Consequently, 'what Random House did was not censorship … It may have been cowardly or alarmist, or it may have been good business, or it may have been an attempt to avoid trouble that ended up buying trouble. But whatever it was, it doesn't rise to the level of constitutional or philosophical concern'.[15]

This, however, is precisely an example of the narrow definition of censorship against which this book has argued, in which censorship is regarded solely as a matter of cuts, bans, proscriptions, injunctions and prohibitions initiated and executed purely at the state level. Random House is not, of course, a state censor, nor is there a shred of evidence to suggest any form of state involvement in their decision not to publish the book. But that decision was still an act of censorship, and the fact that other publishers have subsequently brought it out does not alter that fact one iota. Furthermore, it is a decision which speaks volumes about how attitudes to free speech (and thus to censorship too) have changed since *The Satanic Verses*; as Kenan Malik rightly puts it: 'The fatwa has effectively been internalised'.[16]

Whereas formerly it could be more or less safely assumed that liberal-minded people regarded freedom of expression as an intrinsic good, now many of them regard it as a problem in that it can harm and offend, and thus needs to be curtailed. This is particularly the case, so the argument runs, in an ethnically diverse society containing a wide variety of deeply held views and beliefs, many of which are incompatible but all of which are valid in their own right. As Tariq Modood has put it: 'If people are to occupy the same political space without conflict, they mutually have to limit the extent to which they subject each other's fundamental beliefs to criticism'.[17] On the other hand, it could equally well be argued that in diverse and heterogeneous societies, disagreement is not only bound to occur but is also necessary to ensure a healthy polity. This, certainly, is the view taken by Kenan Malik:

> Far from mutually limiting the extent to which we subject each other's beliefs to criticism, we have to recognise that in a plural society it is both inevitable and important that people offend others. Inevitable, because where different beliefs are deeply held, clashes are unavoidable. And we should deal with those clashes in the open rather than suppress them. Important because any kind of social progress requires one to offend some deeply held sensibilities. 'If liberty means anything', as George Orwell once put it, 'it means the right to tell people what they do not want to hear'.[18]

And this, of course, applies just as much to Muslims and to members of other minority communities as it does to those in the majority community. Free and open discourse – and, crucially, the conditions which allow such discourse to take place – are in the interests of everyone, and not least of those who find their views habitually misrepresented, marginalised or suppressed.

Communication rights

But why, it must finally be asked, is freedom of expression so very important? The classic liberal answer used to be that free media were vital means of keeping state power in check. Now the liberal answer would be rather broader, stressing that freedom of expression is necessary if people are to be informed, to think and decide for themselves, and generally to function fully as citizens of a democratic society.[19]

However, as we saw in chapter 6, the modern media frequently stand accused of failing to provide the democratic goods, focussing instead on lowest common denominator content simply in the interests of profit maximisation. In such a situation, the media's claim that their right to freedom of expression stems from their democratic function is inevitably seriously weakened. However, in recent times, in both the US and Britain, the notion of media freedom seems increasingly to have been re-interpreted by media owners and their apologists as their right to do just as they will with their media regardless of the implications for democracy – in other words, primarily as a property right.

Ranged against this corporate view of media freedom are those who regard it as creating and protecting a social right to a diverse media, a right to be enjoyed by all citizens equally in the interests of a properly functioning democracy, and who argue that the freedom of speech of the many is actually being severely limited by the property rights of the few. In this view of things, media freedom is less about the rights of media owners to communicate and more about the rights of audiences to be informed and to be able to access a wide range of views. At issue, then, is the access of audiences to information and not simply the access of a select few to the means of media production and distribution.

This brings us on to the increasingly important notion of 'communication rights'.

Article 19 of the 1948 Universal Declaration of Human Rights states that 'everyone has the right to freedom of opinion and expression; this right includes freedom to hold opinions without interference, and to seek, receive and impart information and ideas through any media and regardless of frontiers'. This establishes not simply a right to information but a right to communicate, although it was not until the late 1970s that it really came to be understood as such. It was at this time that debates within the Non-aligned Movement about Western media imperialism gave rise to demands for what came to be known as the New World Information and Communication Order. These were articulated at an international level via the United Nations Education, Science and Cultural Organisation (UNESCO), which in 1977 established the International Commission for the Study of Communication Problems under the chairmanship of Seán MacBride. In 1980 this produced a report entitled *Many Voices One World*. Usually known as the *MacBride Report*, this argued that 'communication is a basic individual right, as well as a collective one required by all communities and nations. Freedom of information – and, more specifically the right to seek, receive and impart information – is a fundamental human right; indeed, a prerequisite for many others'.[20] In this respect, one of its key conclusions was that: 'Communication needs in a democratic society should be met by the extension of specific rights such as the right to be informed, the right to inform, the right to privacy, the right to participate in public communication – all elements of a new concept, the right to communicate'.[21]

In more recent years, the need for the democratisation of dominant forms of media, as well as for the development of alternative forms, has been stressed by an extremely wide range of civil society groups – and by no means simply in the developing world. This has given renewed impetus to the debate about communication rights, which above all involves recognising that in societies, and indeed in a world, where power and control over communication resources are distributed extremely unevenly, the notion of freedom of expression involves more than simply the right to communicate and encompasses people's rights to access and participate in diverse and independent media.

Unfortunately, in this struggle for freedom of expression in the broadest sense, which in turn entails struggling against the kinds of market censorship explored in chapters 5 and 6, the mainstream media may well be part of the problem as opposed to part of the solution. Thus, for example, the response of the mainstream British and American media to the *MacBride Report* was to accuse its authors of advocating state control of the media. Now, whilst the Report was not without its problems, this attack on it was motivated entirely by fury at the non-aligned countries for attempting to exercise a degree of control over their own media markets (and so lessen the control of US companies). Indeed, such was the sheer rage generated by the Report that the US left UNESCO in 1985, followed by Britain in 1986.

Meanwhile, when, after very considerable industry lobbying, the FCC in America relaxed its ownership rules in 1996, thus introducing the most sweeping changes in telecommunications law in more than fifty years and drastically altering how the media industry is structured, media coverage of this issue of fundamental importance to the democratic process in America was extremely sparse. One study found that in the nine months between the introduction of the bill and its passing, the three major television networks carried only twelve stories about it, totalling just 19.5 minutes of coverage. Furthermore, most of these stories concerned not the relaxation of ownership regulations but the introduction of new rating and filtering systems. The Republican Senator John McCain was indeed correct when he stated on the floor of the Senate that: 'You will not see this story on any television or hear it on any radio broadcast because it directly affects them'. And when in 2003 the FCC again liberalised these rules, a detailed study by the *American Journalism Review* concluded that most newspaper and broadcast outlets owned by the big media corporations barely mentioned the issue.

However, in spite of this media blackout, the growth of a media oligopoly is a matter of increasing public concern in the US, thanks largely to campaigns waged by bodies such as Freepress, Fairness and Accuracy in Reporting (FAIR) and the Media and Democracy Programme of Common Cause. A significant indication of how successful these campaigns have become is that on Fox News, Bill O'Reilly attacked the thousands who attended the National Conference for Media Reform in Minneapolis in 2007 as 'loons to be ignored', 'unstable people', a 'threat', 'fascists', as being intolerant of dissent and 'doing a lot of damage to America'.[22] Clearly, it's not only in developing countries that criticism of the dominant media is regarded by some as akin to treason.

The moral of this story, however, is most certainly not that the notion of media freedom no longer matters because it has been abused by media corporations to justify the expansion of their empires and the rights of owners to do with their media what they will. It is that the notion of media freedom needs to be greatly expanded so as to take into account the interests of citizens and society as well as of media producers. It also means acknowledging frankly that there are occasions when the media are not the victims of censorship but its agents. The notion of media freedom based on a nineteenth-century model in which a free press was seen as a bulwark against an overweening state and a champion of the powerless really does need seriously re-thinking in order to take account of the fact that the modern media in general, and the press and broadcasting organisations in particular, are now themselves some of the most powerful insti-tutions in society. The media are not simply observers of or commentators on the political process but primary actors within it. They may not tell us what to think (much as many media organisations would like to do so), but they certainly play a key role in defining the key issues of the day and in shaping public attitudes towards them. Greater democracy in the media, however, is best achieved by empowering the powerless and not by muzzling the powerful. Why? Because freedom of expression is a good in itself and an indivisible principle. Because history demonstrates all too clearly that censorship is used just as frequently, if not more frequently, against the powerless and marginal as against the dominant and mighty. And because, post 9/11 and 7/7, the last thing that the coinage of civil liberties needs now is yet more clipping.

Endnotes

Introduction

1. D. Jones, (ed.), *Censorship: a World Encyclopedia*, vols 1–4 (London and Chicago: Fitzroy Dearborn Publishers, 1990).
2. Ibid., p. xi.
3. M. Barker and J. Petley (eds), *Ill Effects: the Media/Violence Debate* (London: Routledge, 1997, 2001); D. Gauntlett, *Moving Experiences: Media Effects and Beyond* (Eastleigh: John Libbey Publishing, 2005, second edition); A. Millwood Hargrave and S. Livingstone, *Harm and Offence in Media Content: a Review of the Evidence* (Bristol: Intellect, 2009, second edition).

Chapter 1

1. M. Aston, *England's Iconoclasts* (Oxford: Clarendon Press, 1988), p. 2.
2. Ibid., p. 4.
3. Ibid., p. 6.
4. Ibid., p. 247.
5. J. Phillips, *The Reformation of Images: Destruction of Art in England, 1535–1660* (Berkeley and Los Angeles, CA: University of California Press, 1973), p. 115.
6. Ibid., p. 186.
7. J. Chang, *Wild Swans: Three Daughters of China* (London: Flamingo, 1993), p. 387.
8. Convocation of the University of Oxford, 'Judgement and Decree'

against 'certain pernicious books and damnable doctrines, destructive to the sacred persons of princes, their State and Government, and of all Human Society', quoted in Green, J., *The Encyclopedia of Censorship* (New York: Facts on File, 1990), p. 27.

9. R.J. Evans, *The Coming of the Third Reich* (London: Allen Lane, 2003), p. 376.

10. Ibid., p. 429.

11. K.P. Fischer, *Nazi Germany: a New History* (New York: The Continuum Publishing Company, 1996), p. 366.

12. M. Ruthven, *A Satanic Affair: Salman Rushdie and the Rage of Islam* (London: Chatto & Windus, 1990), p. 103.

Chapter 2

1. J. Green, *The Encyclopedia of Censorship*, p. 143.

2. Ibid., p. 143.

3. C. Hill, *The Collected Essays of Christopher Hill. Volume 1: Writing and Revolution in 17th Century England* (Brighton: The Harvester Press, 1985), pp. 32–3).

4. J. Milton, *Complete English Poems, Of Education, Areopagitica*. London: J.M. Dent & Sons Ltd, 1990 [1644]), 609–10.

5. C. Hill, *The Collected Essays of Christopher Hill*, p. 51.

6. N. De Jongh, *Prudery and Perversions: the Censoring of the English Stage 1901–1968* (London: Methuen, 2000), p. 18.

7. J. Johnston, *The Lord Chamberlain's Blue Pencil* (London: Hodder & Stoughton,1990), p. 26.

8. J. Green, *The Encyclopedia of Censorship*, p. 175.

9. N. De Jongh, *Prudery and Perversions*, p. 24.

10. Ibid., p. 26.

11. J. Johnston, *The Lord Chamberlain's Blue Pencil*, p. 50.

12. Ibid., p. 52.

13. N. De Jongh, *Prudery and Perversions*, pp. 43–4.

14. Ibid.

15. Ibid., p. 66.

16. Ibid., p. 68.

17. Ibid., p. 110.

18. Ibid., p. 193.

19. J. Johnston, *The Lord Chamberlain's Blue Pencil*, p. 205.

20. N. De Jongh, *Prudery and Perversions*, p. 123.

21. Ibid., pp. 215–6.

22. Ibid., p. 240.

Chapter 3

1. F. Miller, *Censored Hollywood: Sex, Sin & Violence on Screen* (Atlanta GA: Turner Publishing, Inc., 1994), p. 24.

2. G.S. Jowett, "'A capacity for evil": the 1915 Supreme Court *Mutual* Decision', in Bernstein, M. (ed.). *Controlling Hollywood: Censorship and Regulation in the Studio Era* (London: The Athlone Press, 2000) p. 22.

3. Ibid., pp. 22–3.

4. N.M. Hunnings, *Film Censors and the Law* (London: George Allen & Unwin Ltd, 1967), p. 166.

5. J. Green, *The Encyclopedia of Censorship*, p. 334.

6. G.S. Jowett, "A capacity for evil", pp. 27–8.

7. N.M. Hunnings, *Film Censors and the Law*, p. 154.

8. Ibid., p. 155.

9. J. Lewis, *Hollywood v. Hard Core* (New York: New York University Press, 2000), p. 301.

10. F. Miller, *Censored Hollywood*, p. 41.

11. The Code is reproduced in full in J.L. Leff and J.L. Simmons, *The Dame in the Kimono: Hollywood, Censorship and the Production Code* (Lexington KY: The University Press of Kentucky, 2001), pp. 286–90; and in J. Lewis, *Hollywood v. Hard Core*, pp. 302–7.

12. J.L. Leff and J.L. Simmons, *The Dame in the Kimono*, pp. 292–300.

13. F. Miller, *Censored Hollywood*, pp. 75–6.

14. Ibid., p. 79.

15. Ibid., pp. 81–2.
16. N.M. Hunnings, *Film Censors and the Law*, p. 159.
17. J.L. Leff and J.L. Simmons, *The Dame in the Kimono*, p. 115.
18. F. Miller, *Censored Hollywood*, p. 120.
19. J.L. Leff and J.L. Simmons, *The Dame in the Kimono*, pp. 158, 164.
20. F. Miller, *Censored Hollywood*, pp. 150–1.
21. Ibid., p. 189.
22. F. Miller, *Censored Hollywood*, p. 212.
23. J.L. Leff and J.L. Simmons, *The Dame in the Kimono*, pp. 1, 274.
24. F. Miller, *Censored Hollywood*, p. 241.
25. M. Heins, *Sex, Sin, and Blasphemy: a Guide to America's Censorship Wars* (New York: The New Press, 1998), p. 58.

Chapter 4

1. N.M. Hunnings, *Film Censors and the Law*, p. 54.
2. G. Robertson and A. Nicol, *Media Law* (London: Penguin, 2008), p. 820.
3. Ibid., p. 820.
4. Ibid., p. 824.
5. G. Robertson, *Freedom, the Individual and the Law* (London: Penguin, 1993), p. 263.
6. N. Pronay, 'The political censorship of films in Britain between the wars', in Pronay N, and Spring D.W. (eds). *Propaganda, Politics and Film* (London: Macmillan, 1982), p. 114.
7. Ibid., p. 115.
8. N.M. Hunnings, *Film Censors and the Law,*, p. 132.
9. Ibid., p. 133.
10. The full list can be found in ibid., pp. 408–9.
11. J. Trevelyan, *What the Censor Saw* (London: Michael Joseph, 1973), pp. 35–6.
12. Ibid., pp. 37–8.
13. Ibid., p. 41.
14. Ibid., p. 44.

15. All quotations in this section are taken from J. Petley, 'Britain: anti-Nazi films', in Jones, D. (ed.). *Censorship: a World Encyclopedia*, vol. 1 (London and Chicago: Fitzroy Dearborn Publishers, 2001), pp. 331–3.

16. N. Pronay, 'The political censorship of films in Britain between the wars', p. 109.

17. Ibid., p. 122.

18. J. Robertson, *The Hidden Cinema: British Film Censorship in Action, 1913–1975* (London: Routledge, 1989), p. 105.

19. Ibid., p. 108.

20. Ibid., p. 114.

21. N. Rose, *Governing the Soul: the Shaping of the Private Self* (London: Free Association Books, 1999), pp. 1–2.

22. The best accounts of the genesis of this measure are M. Barker, *The Video Nasties: Freedom and Censorship in the Media* (London: Pluto, 1984) and D. Kerekes, and D. Slater, *See No Evil: Banned Films and Video Controversy* (Manchester: Headpress, 2000); the latter also covers its consequences and later history.

23. For further details of this practice see J. Petley, '"Snuffed out": nightmares in a trading standards officer's brain', in Mendik, X. and Harper, G. *Unruly Pleasures: the Cult Film and its Critics* (Guildford: FAB Press, 2000), pp. 205–19.

24. For further discussion of this topic see J. Petley, 'In defence of "video nasties"', in the *British Journalism Review*, 5: 3, pp. 52–7. This is reprinted in O'Sullivan, T and Jewkes, Y. (eds), *The Media Studies Reader* (London: Edward Arnold, 1994), pp. 188–95; and Barker, M. and Petley, J. (eds), *Ill Effects: the Media/Violence Debate*.

25. British Board of Film Classification, *Annual Report 1996–97* (London: BBFC, 1997), Appendix IV: 1.

26. Ibid., pp. 17–18.

27. Ibid., p. 18.

28. The fullest account of this neglected but extremely significant story can be found in J. Petley, 'The censor and the state: or why *Horny Catbabe* matters', in the *Journal of Popular British Cinema*, 3,

pp. 92–103, which cites confidential BBFC documents to demonstrate the full extent of Home Office activity in this saga.

Chapter 5

1. H. Rheingold, *The Virtual Community: Homesteading on the Electronic Frontier*, Cambridge (MA: MIT Press, 1993), p. 7.
2. http://homes.eff.org/~barlow/Declaration-Final.html
3. M. Castells, *The Internet Galaxy: Reflections on the Internet, Business and Society* (Oxford: Oxford University Press, 2001), p. 168.
4. http://www.wiareport.org/index.php/56/blogger-arrests
5. For a useful technical summary of how filtering and blocking systems actually work see B. Esler, 'Filtering, blocking and rating: chaperones or censorship?', in Klang, M. and Murray, A. (eds), *Human Rights in the Digital Age* (London: The GlassHouse Press/Routledge, 2005), pp. 99–110. For more detailed accounts see R. Deibert, J. Palfrey, R. Rohozinski and J. Zittrain, *Access Denied: the Practice and Policy of Global Internet Filtering* (Cambridge MA: The MIT Press, 2008).
6. Human Rights Watch, *Race to the Bottom: Corporate Complicity in Chinese Internet Censorship* (New York NY: Human Rights Watch, 2006), p. 9. Also available at http://www.hrw.org/reports/2006/china0806/
7. Ibid., pp. 18–19.
8. Ibid., p. 12.
9. For lists of banned words and topics drawn up by those campaigning against Internet censorship in China see Ibid., Appendix I and II.
10. Ibid., pp. 13–14.
11. R. Deibert, J. Palfrey, R. Rohozinski and J. Zittrain, *Access Denied: the Practice and Policy of Global Internet Filtering*, p. 266.
12. R. Deibert and N. Villeneuve, 'Firewalls and power: an overview of global state censorship of the internet', in Klang, M. and

Murray, A. (eds), *Human Rights in the Digital Age* (London: The GlassHouse Press/Routledge, 2005), p. 116.

13. J. Goldsmith and T. Wu, *Who Controls the Internet? Illusions of a Borderless World* (Oxford: Oxford University Press, 2006), p. 10.

14. Ibid.

15. R. Faris, S. Wang, J. Palfrey, 'Censorship 2.0', in *Innovations: Technology, Governance, Globalization*, 3: 2, pp. 170, 171. Also available at: http://www.mitpressjournals.org/doi/pdfplus/10.1162/itgg.2008.3.2.165?cookieSet=1

16. Human Rights Watch, *Race to the Bottom: Corporate Complicity in Chinese Internet Censorship*, p. 6.

17. Home Affairs Committee, *Computer Pornography* (London: HMSO, 1994), p. v.

18. Ibid., p. xv.

19. T. Craig and J. Petley, 'Invasion of the Internet abusers', in Barker, M. and Petley, J. (eds), *Ill Effects: the Media/Violence Debate* (London: Routledge, 2001, second edition), p. 191.

20. M. Heins, *Not in Front of the Children: 'Indecency', Censorship and the Corruption of Youth* (New Brunswick NJ: Rutgers University Press, 2007), p. 160.

21. Ibid., pp. 177–8.

22. Y. Akdeniz, *Sex on the Net: the Dilemma of Policing Cyberspace* (Reading: Garnet Publishing, 1999), p. 30.

23. http://www.law.cornell.edu/supct/html/03–218.ZS.html

24. http://www.paed.uscourts.gov/documents/opinions/07D0346P.pdf

25. J. Goldsmith and T. Wu, *Who Controls the Internet?* p. 73.

26. The alarming extent to which this now happens globally is well summarised both by J. Goldsmith and T. Wu, *Who Controls the Internet?*, and by N. Villeneuve, 'Evasion tactics', in *Index on Censorship*, 36: 4, 2007, pp. 71–85.

27. http://www.cyber-rights.org/documents/themet.htm

28. A. Travis, *Bound and Gagged: a Secret History of Obscenity in Britain* (London: Profile Books, 2000), p. 297.

29. http://www.iwf.org.uk/public/page.103.htm

30. Sentencing Guidelines Secretariat, *Sexual Offences Act 2003: Definitive Guidelines* (London, 2007) p. 109.
31. http://www.iwf.org.uk/public/page.103.htm
32. Y. Akdeniz, 'Child pornography', in Akdeniz, Y., Walker, C. and Wall, D. (eds), *The Internet, Law and Society* (Harlow: Longman, 2000), p. 246.
33. L. O'Toole, *Pornocopia: Porn, Sex, Technology and Desire* (London: Serpent's Tail, 1999, second edition), p. 264.
34. Y. Akdeniz, 'Child pornography', p. 248.
35. http://www.ispa.org.uk/press_office/page_58.html

Chapter 6

1. B. Franklin, *Television Policy: the MacTaggart Lectures* (Edinburgh: Edinburgh University Press, 2005), p. 138.
2. For a useful survey of the beginnings of broadcasting 'deregulation' in Europe see J. Petley and G. Romano, 'After the deluge: public service television in Western Europe', in Dowmunt, T. (ed.), *Channels of Resistance: Global Television and Local Empowerment* (London: British Film Institute, 1993).
3. G. Doyle, *Media Ownership* (London: Sage, 2002) pp. 171–2.
4. J. Barron, 'Access to the press; a new First Amendment right', in McChesney, R. (ed.), *Our Unfree Press: 100 Years of Radical Media Criticism* (New York NY: The New Press, 2004), p. 375.
5. http://epic.org/free_speech/red_lion.html
6. C. Baker, *Media Concentration and Democracy: Why Ownership Matters* (Cambridge: Cambridge University Press, 2007), p. 8.
7. Ibid., p. 26.
8. Ibid., p. 16.
9. Ibid., p. 126.
10. Ibid., p. 262.
11. D. Croteau and W. Hoynes, *The Business of Media: Corporate Media and the Public Interest* (Thousand Oaks CA: Pine Forge Press. 2006,

second edition), p. 27.

12. S.C. Jansen, *Censorship: the Knot That Binds Power and Knowledge* (Oxford: Oxford University Press, 1991), p. 168.

13. A process described in detail in R. Greenslade, *Press Gang: How Newspapers Make Profits from Propaganda* (London: Macmillan, 2003), pp.557–65.

14. R. McChesney, *The Political Economy of Media: Enduring Issues, Emerging Dilemmas* (New York NY: Monthly Review Press, 2008), pp. 255–6.

15. C. Baker, Media Concentration and Democracy, p. 2.

16. J. Curran and J. Seaton, *Power Without Responsibility: the Press, Broadcasting and New Media in Britain* (London: Routledge, 2003, sixth edition) p. 350.

17. S. Barnett and I. Gaber, *Westminster Tales: The Twenty-first-century Crisis in Political Journalism* (London: Continuum, 2001), p. 6.

18. J. Curran and J. Seaton, *Power Without Responsibility*, pp. 347–8.

19. For numerous examples of this process at work in the US see B. Bagdikian, *The Media Monopoly* (Boston MA: Beacon Press, 2004, new edition).

20. An excellent account of which is provided by L. Melvern, *The End of the Street* (London: Methuen, 1986).

21. For a useful study of shrinking local news in the UK see B. Franklin, *Local Journalism and Local Media: Making the Local News* (London: Routledge, 2006, second edition).

22. B. Franklin, *Television Policy: the MacTaggart Lectures*, p. 138.

23. *Report of the Committee on Broadcasting* (London: HMSO, 1960), pp. 17–18.

24. For a fuller discussion of 'merit goods' and 'market failure' in broadcasting see A. Graham, 'Broadcasting policy in the multimedia age', in Graham A. et al., *Public Purposes in Broadcasting: Funding the BBC* (Luton: University of Luton Press, 1999); and D. Lipsey, 'In defence of public service broadcasting', in Collins, P. (ed.), *Culture or Anarchy: the Future of Public Service Broadcasting* (London:

The Social Market Foundation, 2002).

25. S. Barnett and E. Seymour, *'A Shrinking Iceberg Travelling South ...'. Changing Trends in British Television: a Case Study of Drama and Current Affairs* (London: Campaign for Quality Television, 1999), p. 72.

26. C. Dover and S. Barnett, *The World on the Box: International Issues in News and Factual Programmes on UK Television 1975–2003* (London: Third World and Environmental Broadcasting Project, 2004), p. 3.

27. J. Keane, *The Media and Democracy* (Cambridge: Polity, 1991), p. 89.

28. D. Smythe, *Dependency Road: Communications, Capitalism, Consciousness and Control* (Norwood NJ: Ablex, 1981), p. 235.

29. M. Hollingsworth, *The Press and Political Dissent: a Question of Censorship*, (London: Pluto Press, 1986), pp. 18–19.

30. This process has been widely documented, but two of the best accounts are in B. Page, *The Murdoch Archipelago* (London: Simon & Schuster, 2003); and R. Belfield, C. Hird and S. Kelly, *Murdoch: the Great Escape* (London: Warner Books, 1994).

31. J. Curran and J. Seaton, *Power Without Responsibility*, p. 70.

32. H. Evans, *Good Times, Bad Times* (Phoenix: London, 1994, third edition), p. 270.

33. Ibid.

34. Ibid.

35. A. Neil, *Full Disclosure* (Pan Books: London, 1996), p. 202.

36. B. Dover, *Rupert's Adventures in China: How Murdoch Lost a Fortune and Found a Wife* (Edinburgh: Mainstream Publishing, 2008), p. 149.

37. Ibid., p. 204.

38. J. Curran and J. Seaton, *Power Without Responsibility*, pp. 83–4.

39. M. Hollingsworth, *The Press and Political Dissent*, p. 25.

40. Ibid., p. 26.

41. A. Neil, *Full Disclosure*, p. 528.

42. Ibid., pp. 543–4.

43. Ibid., p. 544.

44. B. Dover, *Rupert's Adventures in China*, p. 18.

45. Ibid., p. 29.

46. Ibid., p. 153.

47. Ibid., p. 154.

48. Ibid., p. 102.

49. Ibid., p. 230.

50. B. Page, *The Murdoch Archipelago*, p. 406.

51. Ibid., p. 482.

52. For accounts of this campaign see N. Davies, *Flat Earth News* (London: Chatto & Windus, 2008), pp. 304–11; and R. Bolton, *Death on the Rock and Other Stories* (London: W.H. Allen/ Optomen, 1990), pp. 189–306.

53. A. Neil, *Full Disclosure*, pp. 300–10.

54. B. Page, *The Murdoch Archipelago*, p. 414.

55. Ibid., p. 382.

56. Ibid., p. 452.

57. A. Stille, *The Sack of Rome: How a Beautiful European Country with a Fabled History and a Storied Culture Was Taken Over by a Man Named Silvio Berlusconi* (New York NY: Penguin Press, 2006), p. 60.

58. P. Ginsborg, *Silvio Berlusconi: Television, Power and Patrimony* (London: Verso, 2004), p. 51.

59. A. Stille, *The Sack of Rome*, p. 60.

60. Ibid., p. 167.

61. Ibid., p. 184.

62. T. Jones, *The Dark Heart of Italy* (London: Faber and Faber, 2007, revised edition), p. 126.

63. P. Statham, 'Berlusconi, the media and the new Right in Italy', in *Press/Politics* 1: 1, pp. 87–105, 1996, p. 96.

64. T. Jones, *The Dark Heart of Italy*, p. 108.

Conclusion

1. R. Dworkin, 'A new map of censorship', in *Words and Deeds: Incitement, Hate Speech and the Right to Free Expression* (London: Index on Censorship, 2005), p. 4.
2. Ibid., p. 5.
3. G. Robertson and A. Nicol, *Media Law*, p. 44.
4. Ibid., p. 80.
5. Ibid., p. 52.
6. Ibid., p. 65.
7. *New Statesman*, 'Citizen 2.0: Protecting Privacy, Security and Civil Liberties in a Digital Society'. Insert to *New Statesman*, 4 August, 2008, p. 15.
8. http://www.firstamendmentcenter.org/faclibrary/casesummary.aspx?case=Whitney_v_CA
9. http://www.firstamendmentcenter.org/faclibrary/casesummary.aspx?case=Whitney_v_CA)
10. http://www.guardian.co.uk/uk/2000/apr/11/irving1
11. http://news.bbc.co.uk/1/hi/world/europe/4733820.stm
12. http://news.bbc.co.uk/1/hi/uk/4578534.stm
13. Kenan Malik, 'Shadow of the fatwa', in *Index on Censorship*, 37: 4, 2008, p. 114.
14. http://www.randomhouse.com/rhpg/medinaletter.html
15. http://fish.blogs.nytimes.com/2008/08/24/crying-censorship/
16. Kenan Malik, 'Shadow of the fatwa', p. 115.
17. Ibid., p. 118.
18. Ibid., p. 119.
19. For a critical account of the arguments for freedom of expression see J. Petley, *Censoring the Word* (Oxford: Seagull Books, 2007) and N. Warburton, *Free Speech: A Very Short Introduction* (Oxford: Oxford University Press, 2009).

20. MacBride Commission, *Many Voices, One World: Towards a New, More Just, and More Efficient World Information and Communication Order* (Lanham, MD: Rowman & Littlefield, 2004), p. 253.

21. Ibid., p. 265.

22. https://secure.freepress.net/site/Advocacy?cmd=display&page=User Action&id=269

Index